Fairey Firefly
in action

By W. A. Harrison

Color by Don Greer and David Gebhardt

Line art by Darren Glenn

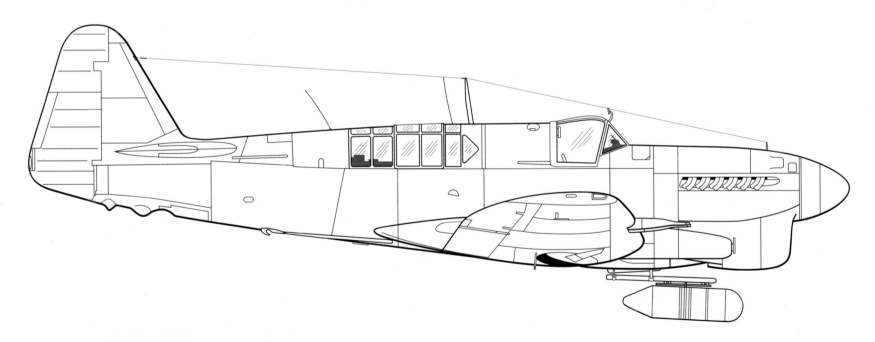

2/15   5/10

MW00611115

Squadron Signal®
Publications

Aircraft Number 200

Cover: Lt. D. Levitt, RNVR, of the Fleet Air Arm's 1770 Squadron, shoots down a Ki-43 *Hayabusa* **during a strike on targets at Pangkalan Brandan in Northern Sumatra on 4 January 1945. It was 1770 Squadron's first aerial combat victory of World War II. Later that month, Lt. Levitt was killed during an attack on a Japanese oil refinery at Palembang, Sumatra.**

Copyright 2006 Squadron/Signal Publications
1115 Crowley Drive, Carrollton, Texas 75006-1312 U.S.A.
Printed in the U.S.A.

All rights reserved. No part of this publication may be reproduced, stored in a retrieval system, or transmitted in any form by means electrical, mechanical, or otherwise, without written permission of the publisher.

ISBN 0-89747-501-1

If you have any photographs of aircraft, armor, soldiers or ships of any nation, particularly wartime snapshots, why not share them with us and help make Squadron/Signal's books all the more interesting and complete in the future? Any photograph sent to us will be copied and the original returned. The donor will be fully credited for any photos used. Please send them to:

Squadron/Signal Publications
1115 Crowley Drive
Carrollton, TX 75006-1312 U.S.A.
www.SquadronSignalPublications.com

About the In Action Series

"In Action" books, despite the title of the genre, are books tracing the development of a single type of aircraft, armored vehicle, or ship from prototype to the final production variant. Experimental or "one-off" variants can also be included. Our first "In Action" book was printed in 1971.

Acknowledgements

David Masters
Imperial War Museum
RAF Museum
Royal Australian Navy
Canadian Department of Defence
Royal Danish Air Force
Royal Netherlands Navy
Indian Navy

Dedication:

To all the crews that flew the Firefly and the memories of those who lost their lives while doing so.

A Note on Designations

The British aircraft designation system uses the airplane's official name as a part. The full designation consists of the name, a letter or set of letters indicating the role or mission, and a mark number. In a few cases the mark number is followed by a letter indicating a modification. Before World War II, mark numbers, written in Roman numerals, were used alone without the role letters. The role letters were added during the war. Following the war, Arabic numerals replaced Roman numerals. In this work, Arabic numerals are used throughout for ease of reading, although the wartime Fireflies' designations actually used Roman numerals.

▸ **The classic lines of the Firefly FR.1 are shown here by DK418, which joined 790 Squadron at Charlton Horethorne in December 1944. This is a late production model with the raised pilot's cockpit windshield and canopy.**

Introduction

The Fairey Firefly, one of the most underrated strike fighters of World War II, was the result of numerous changes to its original specifications over an extended period. Such a lengthy and protracted development was characterisitc of the British aircraft industry's relationship to the British government. In those days the British Air Ministry controlled all orders for aircraft, including those for their naval Fleet Air Arm (FAA), and developed specifications in response to the requirements of the armed services. These specifications were then issued to the aircraft industry. In response, there might be design submissions from a half-dozen British aircraft manufacturers, all hoping for orders, and the Air Ministry had the luxury of picking the winner, often from among two or more prototypes of aircraft which potentially suited the needs of the service requiring them. Such was the case with the Fairey Firefly.

The original Air Ministry specification N.8/39 for a two-seat front-gun naval fighter, and N.9/39 for a similar aircraft but with a powered gun turret behind the pilot's cockpit (not unlike the Blackburn Skua and Boulton Paul Defiant), resulted in the Ministry's receiving submissions from five companies, including the Fairey Aviation Company. Fairey was in a fortunate position, as they had supplied aircraft for naval purposes (Flycatcher, IIIF, Seal, Seafox, Swordfish, Albacore, and Fulmar) for many years. Initial designs to meet the specification were submitted by Marcelle Lobelle, Fairey's chief designer, but he left Fairey in 1939 to form his own company, and H. E. Chaplin (known to all and sundry as 'Charlie'), who worked in the design office, became Fairey's chief designer. On taking up his new post he immediately swept Lobelle's designs aside and started fresh, suggesting utilizing one design for both roles. The first design, a single-seat fighter, was not unlike the Supermarine Spitfire, and the other, a two-seat fleet strike-fighter, was intended as a replacement for the slow Fairey Fulmar. The Air Ministry did not like Chaplin's idea but eventually gave the go-ahead on a new two-seat naval fighter to be built by Fairey under a revised specification N.5/40F. The single-seat fighter project went to Blackburn, who eventually produced it as the 'Firebrand.' Two prototypes, eleven development aircraft, and 187 production machines were ordered to the new specification, with the name 'Firefly' being chosen in December 1940.

It was decided at an early stage that the Firefly, while being produced mainly at Fairey's Hayes factory in Middlesex, would benefit from wartime group production methods. Accordingly, General Aircraft Limited (GAL) at Hanworth and Aero Engines Ltd. of Bristol became subcontractors along with many other minor component companies.

The Ministry of Aircraft Production (MAP) informed Fairey that they were planning to order another 100 Firefly aircraft in addition to the 200 already on order. The first three aircraft, Z1826-1828, were hand-built in the Experimental Shop at Hayes and assembled at the Fairey-owned Great West Aerodrome at Heathrow. On 22 December 1941, the late F/Lt. Christopher S. Staniland, Fairey's Chief Test Pilot, took the first Firefly, Z1826, on its maiden flight. Chris Staniland was at that time every schoolboy's hero — a dashing ex-RAF fighter pilot, winner of numerous motorbike races and records set at tracks such as Brooklands, a racing car driver who drove his own cars and was also in the Riley racing team for four seasons, and a test pilot for one of Britain's best known aviation companies. F/Lt. Staniland found no major problems with the prototype Firefly, and it was suggested that it go straight to the Aeroplane & Armament Experimental Establishment (A. & A.E.E.) at Boscombe Down for trials in an effort to speed up its entry into service. Staniland delivered Z1826 to Boscombe on 28 April 1942 – minus the pilot's canopy, which had come off on the way there.

The unpainted prototype Firefly Z1826 after assembly at Fairey's Great West Aerodrome. The low windshield and pilot's hood and fabric-covered ailerons, elevators, and rudder are clearly evident. Its first flight was on 22 December 1941 in the hands of Fairey test pilot F/Lt Christopher Staniland.

The test pilots at Boscombe Down found the Firefly aileron controls to be light throughout the speed range but "overbalanced," requiring high inputs at low speeds. There was some "snatch" on the elevators, but otherwise they concluded that once the control problems had been overcome, "the aircraft should make a satisfactory naval fighter." The MAP ordered another three hundred Fireflies and said they wanted fifty a month until the end of 1944.

The Firefly program suffered a setback on 26 June 1942 when Chris Staniland was killed test flying the second prototype Firefly, Z1827; he was only thirty-six. The cause has never been satisfactorily explained, but investigators thought it to be a failure of the elevators. Staniland's colleague, F. H. Dixon, took over the flight test program and was later joined by production test pilots Colin Evans and Seth Smith.

The fourth Firefly F. I, Z1829, was delivered to the FAA Service Trials Unit at Arbroath naval base early in 1943. Naval pilots found the Firefly handled well in all aspects but criticized the low windshield and canopy, which restricted the pilot's view when landing. A correction was incorporated on the production line, and later aircraft were delivered with higher windshields and raised cockpit canopies. Carrier deck landing trials were carried out with Firefly F.1 Z1839 aboard the carrier HMS *Illustrious* in May 1943. The pilot, Lt Eric Brown, had a fright during the day when, during his third takeoff, the pilot's canopy became detached and hit the leading edge of the port horizontal stabilizer, severing the main spar. Making a somewhat shaky circuit, Brown used all his skills to land back on the carrier safely. Further trials the following month using Firefly F.1 Z1844 were concluded satisfactorily.

Toward the end of 1943, Firefly F.1 Z1883 was sent to the Naval Air Fighting Development Unit, then based at RAF Wittering, for tactical trials. These revealed that, although the Firefly F.1 had good handling characteristics, it would be more suited for long-range close-escort duties and/or as a naval night fighter, rather than as a straight day combat fighter. The trials also showed that in mock combat with contemporary single seat fighters, the Firefly's turning circle was outstanding when the pilot lowered the flaps to the mid-position. In fact, Firefly F.1 Z1908 was sent to the US for such trials at a Joint Fighter Conference, where it was flown against various British and American fighters, including a captured Japanese Mitsubishi A6M2 Type O 'Zero.' When its flaps were lowered to the mid-position, the Firefly could out-turn the Zero.

All Fireflies built at the Hayes factory were towed (minus wings and tail unit) behind lorries to Fairey's Great West Aerodrome where they were assembled and test flown. The Firefly F.1 was released for squadron use on 7 July 1943 and entered service with the FAA in October 1943. It soon proved itself, initially operating against shipping and shore targets along the Norwegian coast, in attacks on the German battleship *Tirpitz,* and with considerable success operating against Japanese targets with the British Pacific Fleet (BPF) in support of the Allied push toward Japan. The F.1 was followed by the FR.1, which incorporated ASH (air-to-surface homing) radar. Firefly F.1s retrofitted with ASH were known as Firefly F.1As. The Firefly FR.1 was released for service use on 16 February 1945 with the MAP telling Fairey that production of the Firefly 1 would continue into 1946 when the Firefly 4 would replace it.

The Firefly NF.1 night fighter, having Airborne Interception (AI) radar, was developed alongside the F.1 on the production line. After World War II, a number of Firefly 1s were converted to T.1 and T.2 tactical weapons trainers, each fitted with dual controls and a raised rear single cockpit. Some, converted to target-tow aircraft, were known as TT.1. In 1945 a number of Firefly 1s were sold to the Royal Netherlands Navy and were used operationally against terrorists in the Dutch East Indies by the Royal Netherlands Naval Air Service (*Marine Luchtvaardienst*).

The NF.2 was to have been a night fighter with radomes mounted on the wing leading edge, but this model was a failure and did not enter production.

(▶ 8)

▲ **Firefly F.1 Z2035 in 1942 with a black spinner. The Hispano 20 mm cannon are not faired in at this stage. Noticeable is the restricted view of the pilot with the earlier low windshield and lower canopy. The fairings on the mid-trailing edge house the flap linkage mechanism.**

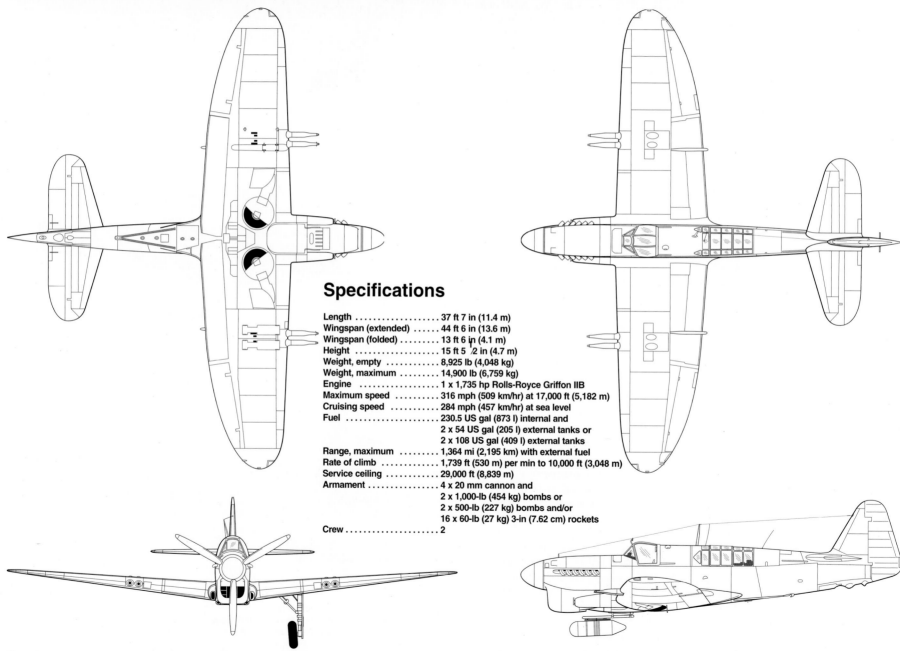

Specifications

Length	37 ft 7 in (11.4 m)
Wingspan (extended)	44 ft 6 in (13.6 m)
Wingspan (folded)	13 ft 6 in (4.1 m)
Height	15 ft 5 1/2 in (4.7 m)
Weight, empty	8,925 lb (4,048 kg)
Weight, maximum	14,900 lb (6,759 kg)
Engine	1 x 1,735 hp Rolls-Royce Griffon IIB
Maximum speed	316 mph (509 km/hr) at 17,000 ft (5,182 m)
Cruising speed	284 mph (457 km/hr) at sea level
Fuel	230.5 US gal (873 l) internal and 2 x 54 US gal (205 l) external tanks or 2 x 108 US gal (409 l) external tanks
Range, maximum	1,364 mi (2,195 km) with external fuel
Rate of climb	1,739 ft (530 m) per min to 10,000 ft (3,048 m)
Service ceiling	29,000 ft (8,839 m)
Armament	4 x 20 mm cannon and 2 x 1,000-lb (454 kg) bombs or 2 x 500-lb (227 kg) bombs and/or 16 x 60-lb (27 kg) 3-in (7.62 cm) rockets
Crew	2

◂ Another view of Z2035 showing in profile the low windshield and pilot's hood. The aircraft's Fairey-Youngman flaps are fully retracted out of the airflow. The thin slot visible above 'ROYAL NAVY' houses the wing retaining arm which locks the folded wing alongside the fuselage.

▸ Firefly FR.1 DK418 showing the Fairey-Youngman flaps in the cruise position. There were four positions for the flaps: HOUSED (fully up), CRUISING (first quadrant), TAKE-OFF (second quadrant), and LAND (fully down). With the flaps at CRUISING they offered maximum maneuverability but could not be used for normal flight.

7

The Firefly F.3 was to have had the more powerful 1,540 hp Rolls-Royce Griffon 61 engine, but problems with longitudinal stability led to its cancellation.

The Firefly FR.4 was a major design change utilizing a 2,005 hp Rolls-Royce Griffon 74 with a four-blade propeller and incorporating leading edge radiators in the center section, clipped wing tips, and a re-profiled nose and tail area. The FAA later converted some FR.4s for target-towing duties as the TT.4. The FR.4 was also purchased by the Royal Netherlands Navy who converted some to NF.4 night fighters and some into TT.4 target-towers. The Firefly FR.5, a multi-role version of the FR.4, was easily converted between the fighter-reconnaissance, night-fighter, or anti-submarine roles and was used with great success as a strike fighter during the Korean War. The Royal Netherlands Naval Air Service ordered the Mk.5 in the night-fighter role, and the Australian Navy used the FR.5 during the Korean War. Later they modified a number of FR.5s as dual-control trainers, the T.5, and as target-towers, known as TT.5, utilizing the same design as the Mk.5.

The Firefly AS.6 was an anti-submarine version with no guns but with a wide range of submarine detection gear and external weapon-carrying capability. The TT.6 was an Australian Navy conversion to the target-towing role.

The Firefly AS.7 saw considerable design changes, fitting a Rolls-Royce Griffon 59, under-nose radiator, re-profiled wings and tail, and large observer's cockpit canopy. In its intended role of anti-submarine aircraft it was a failure, but as a T.7 was used to train observers.

The U.8 was a target drone version of the Mk.7, and the final Firefly, the U.9, was a drone conversion of the Firefly FR.5.

The Firefly was built in three basic models, the Mk.1, Mk.4, and Mk.7; all other models were design changes to these three basic configurations.

Firefly F.1

October 1943 saw the introduction of the Firefly as both a day fighter, the F.1, and as a night-fighter, the NF.1. Both had been developed in parallel on the production line, as the FAA were in desperate need of an operational naval night-fighter. The British Admiralty could not accept the idea of a single-seat fighter filling the roles of strike and reconnaissance without an observer (navigator) along to help the pilot find the carrier again! Consequently, to carry on this tradition, the Firefly incorporated a second cockpit behind the pilot, resulting in an appearance similar to that of its predecessor, the Fairey Fulmar. The Firefly, however, looked much more aggressive with two 20 mm cannon in each wing. Additional armament could be carried, up to two 1,000-pound bombs plus other external stores. Later the mountings for eight three-inch rocket projectiles (R/Ps) were fitted.

Fuselage strength came from twenty-one 'U'-shaped frames within a flush-riveted light alloy monocoque structure; the Firefly had no internal stringers, as the fuselage was built in two separate halves which were joined along a vertical centerline. The forward fuselage contained space for the pilot's cockpit, and a faired-in observer's cockpit was just aft of the wing trailing edge. The pilot's cockpit canopy, consisting of three transparent panels, slid back on rails. The observer's entrance, a transparent panel on the port side, was hinged to the fuselage decking.

Two retractable catapult spools were fitted to the front fuselage. Two rear catapult spools were retractable when not in use, but when the aircraft was launched by catapult, the spools were locked down and could not be retracted after take-off. The deck arrester gear was made up from a transverse torque shaft from which two tubes converged to join the (▶ 10)

The complicated manual wing folding for the Firefly 1s, 4s, and early 5s required a large ground crew. Once the wing lock pins were removed, long rods were attached to the wing tips to pull them upward, backward, and downward so that the tips could be attached to retaining arms on the rear fuselage, seen here being deployed by a crewman on each side. The wing locking stays can be seen already deployed just below the upper wing roundels.

Fairey Firefly Development

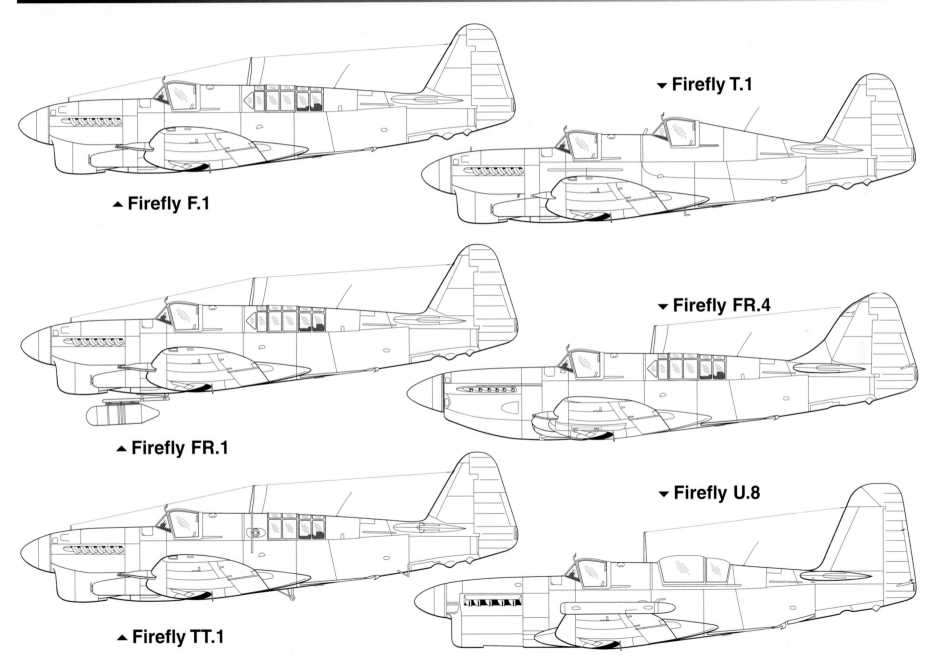

▲ Firefly F.1

▼ Firefly T.1

▲ Firefly FR.1

▼ Firefly FR.4

▲ Firefly TT.1

▼ Firefly U.8

◄ In the post-war period it became normal practice to display the aircraft serial number under the wings in large letters and numerals as seen here on FR.1 PP604. The footstep showing near the fuselage roundel was fully retractable and was stowed in clips at the wing center section root fairing. It was connected to the tail wheel by means of a Bowden cable and was retracted with the tail wheel.

▼ The outer wing was hinged from the rear spar only, swinging up and around so that the flap ended up under the center section. This picture is of Firefly F.1 Z1908 when it was in the U.S. for performance trials during a Joint Fighter Conference. (US Navy)

hook, forming an 'A' frame; the hook was held in a snap clip mounted at the bottom of fuselage frame nineteen. The pilot released the hook via a hook-shaped lever in the cockpit.

A 145-gallon fuel tank was fitted in the fuselage between the two cockpits, and two other tanks of forty-six gallons each were installed in the leading edge of the wing center section, one per side.

The wings were in two sections. The center section structure was a light alloy structure comprised of front and rear spars strengthened by diagonal bracing diaphragms, with eight ribs each side of the centerline, plus oil tank bearers. The inward-retracting landing gear consisted of two shock-absorber struts to which fairings were attached, and was fully enclosed within the center section when retracted. The outer wings housed two electro-pneumatically operated British Hispano 20 mm cannon, the inner guns having 175 rounds per gun, the outer ones 145 rounds. Ailerons and hydraulically-operated Fairey-Youngman flaps were fitted. The flaps were normally stowed in the wing's trailing edge but could be lowered to a mid-position that enhanced maneuverability. The outer wings were hinged at the rear ends of the rear spars and could be folded back manually against the fuselage and secured by a reception sleeve which engaged with a locking stay mounted in the rear fuselage. Attachment points on the wings allowed the carriage of two forty-five-gallon or ninety-gallon long-range tanks or bomb beams to take bombs of up to 1,000 pounds. Four hooks were fitted to each outer wing to take the three-inch R/P plates.

A flush-riveted horizontal stabilizer and fin were attached to the rear fuselage with a fabric-covered rudder. The rudder and elevators had trim tabs and were horn-balanced with the weights bolted to the leading edges of the horn.

Power was provided by a Rolls-Royce Griffon IIB, rated at 1,735 hp at sea level or 1,495 hp at 14,000 feet. It drove a Rotol thirteen-feet diameter, three-blade, variable-pitch propeller with constant-speed control. After the 470th Firefly 1, production switched to the Griffon (►► 14)

▲ The 12-cylinder Rolls-Royce Griffon IIB engine was designed specifically to give high power to low-flying naval aircraft and was chosen as the powerplant for the new Fairey Firefly. The IIB was installed in the first 470 Fireflies, after which the Griffon XII was used. Both engines were rated at 1,735 hp at 1,000 feet, but the Mk. XII had a more powerful supercharger and strengthened reduction gear.

▼ The Fairey-Youngman flaps enhanced the performance of the Firefly and when lowered to the cruise position gave it a definite advantage over other fighters. The flaps allowed a tighter turning circle which, in the hands of a good pilot, could be used to good effect when in combat. (Flight)

▲ A naval pilot and his observer give an idea of the size of the Firefly FR.1. The rocket projectiles (RPs) are fitted on zero-length Mk.VIII carriers which required two saddles to mount each rocket, one forward and one aft. A second tier could be mounted below using a double saddle. These have 60-lb heads, which were painted dark green; those with a white circle were semi-armor piercing, while those with red circles were high-explosive.

▼ The A-frame arresting gear comprised a transverse torque shaft from which two tubes converged at their attachment to the hook. The hook was held by a snap fitting operated by a lever in the cockpit. A damper mounted inside the lower fuselage absorbed the sudden shock imposed on the airframe when catching the arrestor cable. (Flight)

An early production Firefly F.1 was converted into the prototype Firefly NF.2 (Z1831/G) in 1943. It has the usual low windshield and pilot's canopy, unfaired cannon, prototype markings, and anti-spin strakes at the top of the fin. The mock radar nacelles, one on each side, were not a success. Putting radio and radar equipment in the rear cockpit upset the center of gravity, so a fifteen-inch fuselage plug was fitted just forward of the pilot's cockpit. (IWM)

A 1944 view of Z1831/G after the radar nacelles had been shortened. It still was not successful; many of the thirty-seven built were converted to FR.1 status.

The unsuccessful Firefly F.3 resulted from the installation of a Rolls-Royce Griffon 61 in Firefly F.1 Z1835. Intended as a single-seat fighter, the F.3 was cancelled when it was discovered the aircraft suffered from longitudinal instability. The Griffon engine required new exhaust baffles and a larger annular radiator tunnel.

◄ As a follow-up to the failed Firefly NF.2, Z1844, an early production F.1 with low windshield and unfaired cannon, was used by Rolls-Royce for tests to reduce exhaust glare for the Firefly NF.1 night fighter.

▼ Close-up of the Rolls-Royce exhaust glare shield for Firefly night fighters. The project engineer said that he could walk all around the aircraft and not see any exhaust glow. Glare shields were fitted to some Firefly NF.1s following World War II but not to FR.1s.

XII engine which had the same power ratings but used increased supercharger power and had a strengthened reduction gear.

Total production of all Firefly 1s came to 872 aircraft, of which 132 were built under license by General Aircraft Limited at Hanworth, plus thirty taken off the post-war production line for the Royal Netherlands Navy.

Firefly F. 1A

This was essentially a Firefly F.1 converted to FR.1 standard by FAA maintenance units using drawings supplied by Fairey Aviation. When converted, these aircraft were known by the name 'ASHCAT,' but by naval personnel as the 'ASHCAN!' The exact number of aircraft converted to this standard is not known.

Firefly FR. 1

Built in parallel to the F.1 on the production line at Hayes, and later supplanting it, the FR.1's construction and armament was the same as that of the F.1. A deeper windshield, higher pilot's cockpit canopy, and faired-in 20 mm cannons were among a number of changes incorporated. A bomb-shaped radome mounted below the forward fuselage contained ASH (AN/APS-4) radar with appropriate equipment in the observer's cockpit. The FR.1 was released for FAA service on 16 February 1945 and immediately became popular with pilots due to the better visibility afforded by its raised cockpit windshield and canopy. It quickly supplanted the F.1s already in squadron service, and 1770, 1771, and 1772 Squadrons operated them with great success against the Japanese in the

A 1952 in-service view of Firefly FR.1 PP523 '264' of 796 Squadron showing the ASH (air-to surface homing) radar nacelle mounted beneath the engine bay. Although the ASH appears level, it actually points slightly down to clear the propeller arc. The upper fuselage Dark Sea Grey has been extended slightly onto the leading edge of the fin. Note the absence of a fin flash, which was omitted from naval aircraft from the late 1940s.

Far East. It was also used by 805, 812, 814, 816, 822, 824, 825, 826, 827, and 837 Squadrons in front-line service, 1830 and 1841 Reserve Squadrons, and twenty-nine second-line squadrons. The Firefly FR.1 also became the FAA's standard two-seat fighter in the post-World War II era. No. 827 Squadron was still operating the FR.1 as part of the 13th CAG aboard HMS *Triumph* in Far Eastern waters, with Seafire F.47s of 800 Squadron, when the Korean War broke out. They operated until September 1950, by which time only two were fit to fly due to age, usage, and lack of spare parts.

Firefly NF.1

Some 140 Firefly NF.1s were produced on the same production line as the F.1/FR.1, replacing the cancelled Firefly NF.2. In mid-1944 enough ASH (US Navy AN/APS-4) radar sets were available to fit them to a Firefly FR.1 for trials with the Night Fighter Interception Unit (NFIU). It was a compact set which allowed the weighty two hundred pounds to be contained in a bomb-shaped transmitter/receiver pod which was located on a mounting arm under the forward fuselage. Although not as good as the American APS-6 sets, which the US Navy wanted for its own needs, it was an improvement on the A.I Mk.X. The new sets were introduced on the FR.1 production line, but the radar-equipped models were known as Firefly NF.1s. They were flown by 805, 812, 816, 827, 1790, 1791, and 1792 Squadrons and 732, 746, 784, 792 and 794 (second-line) Squadrons.

In 1944 Heinkel He 111 bombers of the 3rd *Gruppen* of *Kampfgeschwader* 3 began air-launching V-1 flying bombs against targets in central England. By the end of November the unit, now known as *Kampfgeschwader* 53, had three Gruppen all air-launching V-1s against Britain. The Naval Fighter Interception Unit (NFIU) at RAF Ford had some Firefly NF.1s (▸ 24)

A pair of Firefly FR.1s of 816 Squadron, which was embarked in HMS *Ocean* during the British withdrawal from Palestine in 1946. In the post-World War II era, tail codes indicated the carrier to which the squadron belonged. The fairing above the ASH nacelle was not standard but could be seen on some aircraft of that era. Under the wings are zero-length rocket launchers.

▲ Firefly NF.1 PP617 of 792 Squadron, a Night Fighter Training Unit based at Culdrose between January 1948 and July 1950. Unusual is the two-tone light and dark gray camouflage pattern with Type 'A' roundels. This aircraft was later converted to a T.3. (BC Lyons)

▲ 746 Squadron used Firefly NF.1s, such as MB564 shown here, to attempt interception of V-1 carrying Heinkel He 111s trying to launch their missiles off the east coast of Britain in 1944-45. The weather was usually poor, and although radar-directed, Fireflies did not shoot down any of the German missile carriers. (J Kneale)

▼ Firefly NF.1 MB590 'W' of 1791 Squadron formates on a sister aircraft for its picture in July 1945. The angle of the ASH installation in relation to the thrust line can be clearly seen. The letter 'W' was yellow.

▼ Firefly F.1 Z1964 displays the approach configuration with flaps and hook down as it arrives at the flight deck. The large post-war underwing serial numbers and wingtip roundels are clearly evident.

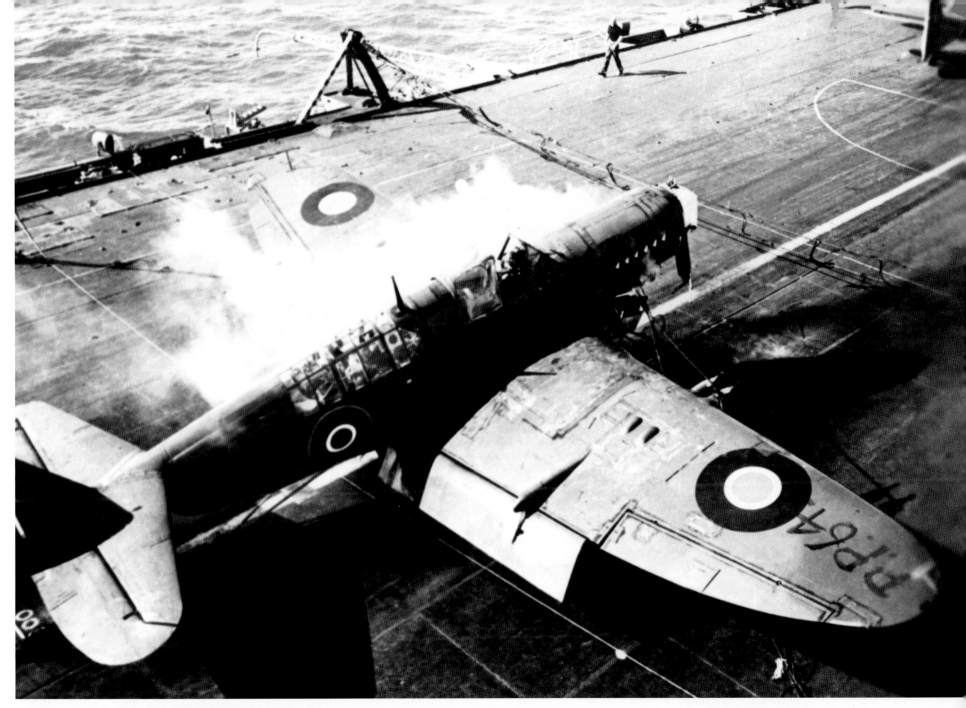

Firefly FR.1 PP645 of 837 Squadron comes to grief in May 1947 as it jumps the wires and ends up in HMS *Glory*'s barrier. The wooden Rotol propeller has shattered, and extensive damage can be seen to the radiator tunnel area. It was rebuilt and flew until May 1954 when it was scrapped.

▲ The first Firefly FR.4 prototype, Z2118. Converted from an FR.1, it is in interim form with the semi-elliptical wings and horizontal stabilizer of the Mk.1 but fitted with leading edge radiators. It has a rounded spinner and a carburetor cooling intake below the nose. A four-blade propeller has been fitted to absorb the increased power of the Rolls-Royce Griffon 74.

▲ Firefly FR.4 prototype, Z2118, now displaying the shorter wing and revised profile of the fin. The spinner is more pointed, and short-barrel 20 mm cannons have replaced the earlier long-barrel weapons. (IWM)

▼ The second prototype Firefly FR.4, MB649, above the clouds and showing off its new lines. It is 'clean,' with no wing tanks or radar nacelles, although a glare shield has been added to the last three exhaust manifolds on the starboard side. Naval aircraft in the immediate post-World War II era were camouflaged in the standard two-tone gray scheme.

▼ MB649, the second prototype Firefly FR.4, displays the undersides and layout of the new mark in this 1946 view. It never entered naval service, instead spending its days as a test aircraft.

▲ An early production Firefly FR.4, TW729 tests the revised nose profile. It was delivered to the Navy on 1 March 1947 and flew with training squadrons until July 1957 when it was sold for scrap.

▲ Firefly FR.4 TW695 was pulled from the production line and fitted with contra-rotating propellers to reduce the torque generated when full power was applied. The Firefly's short throttle travel frequently caused pilots to apply full power when overshooting a poor approach, suddenly creating a torque stall causing the aircraft to end up in the sea. (IWM)

▼ As part of their sales campaign, Fairey used Firefly FR.4 TW692 for tropical trials in 1948. Painted overall pale gray and fitted with four long-range tanks, it visited numerous Middle East countries in an attempt to sell them the Firefly.

▼ Two Firefly FR.4s, TW734 'F' and TW730 'B,' of 825 Squadron at Eglinton in 1948. The ASH nacelle and wing tank were standard fittings on Firefly 4s, 5s, and 6s, although the ASH nacelle could be changed for another wing tank when required. (T. Hughes)

19

▲ The pilot's cockpit of the Firefly FR.4 differed very little from that of earlier variants. Each had slight differences, but these did not affect the overall layout. The bar across the top of the instrument panel in front of the gyro gun sight held a plotting board for the pilot and is shown here in the stowed position.

▲ This low angle picture of a Firefly Mk.4 pilot's cockpit shows the adjustable rudder pedal bar. The upper switch on the control column was for guns, rocket projectiles, and bomb release. The bottom one was an IFF (Identification Friend or Foe) button, pressed when returning to ship or base.

► Firefly TT.4 VH132 airborne out of Ford Naval Air Station for a target-towing detail. The 'G' type Mk.3 winch is clearly seen with its slipstream-driven propeller at the front of its streamlined container. The winch could be jettisoned. Under the center fuselage is the target towing exchange unit Type 'B' Mk. 2, and just aft of that can be seen the end of the launch tube for the drogues. The deck hook and guns have been removed, and the ASH nacelle has been replaced by a fuel tank.

◄ Firefly FR.4 of the Royal Australian Navy converted for the target-towing role with guns removed and a 'G' type winch Mk.3. This one is also fitted with bomb carriers. An exhaust glare shield has been fitted, suggesting that target towing is only one of its duties. (RAN)

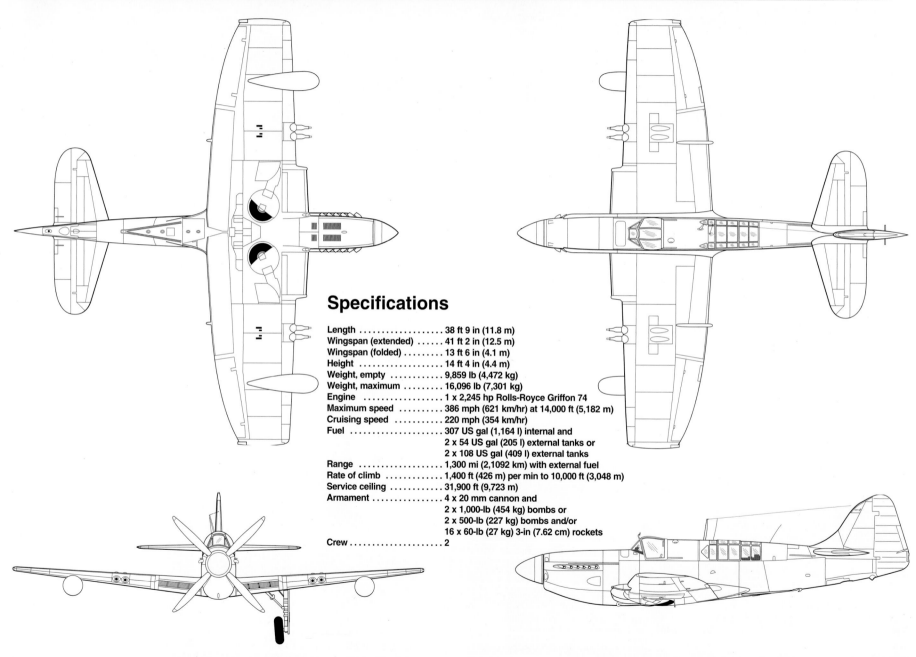

Specifications

Length . . . . 38 ft 9 in (11.8 m)
Wingspan (extended) . . . . . . 41 ft 2 in (12.5 m)
Wingspan (folded) . . . . 13 ft 6 in (4.1 m)
Height . . . . 14 ft 4 in (4.4 m)
Weight, empty . . . . 9,859 lb (4,472 kg)
Weight, maximum . . . . 16,096 lb (7,301 kg)
Engine . . . . 1 x 2,245 hp Rolls-Royce Griffon 74
Maximum speed . . . . 386 mph (621 km/hr) at 14,000 ft (5,182 m)
Cruising speed . . . . 220 mph (354 km/hr)
Fuel . . . . 307 US gal (1,164 l) internal and
2 x 54 US gal (205 l) external tanks or
2 x 108 US gal (409 l) external tanks
Range . . . . 1,300 mi (2,1092 km) with external fuel
Rate of climb . . . . 1,400 ft (426 m) per min to 10,000 ft (3,048 m)
Service ceiling . . . . 31,900 ft (9,723 m)
Armament . . . . 4 x 20 mm cannon and
2 x 1,000-lb (454 kg) bombs or
2 x 500-lb (227 kg) bombs and/or
16 x 60-lb (27 kg) 3-in (7.62 cm) rockets
Crew 2

RATO Installation

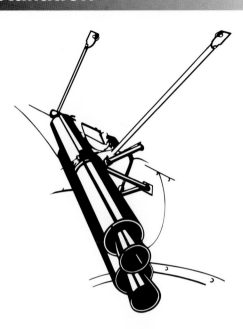

▲ Firefly FR.5 WB333 '239/O' of 810 Squadron approaches HMS *Ocean* on the downwind leg of the landing pattern. The arrestor hook is already lowered. On the flight deck are Hawker Sea Furies and two Grumman AS.4 (TBM-3) Avengers with a Sikorsky Dragonfly hovering just off the starboard side.

▼ RATO gear fitted to a Dutch Navy Firefly FR.5. Use of RATO was not to be taken lightly. One FAA pilot, on firing the rockets, was overtaken on one side by a motor that had broken free and lost half his beard as a result!

Pilot's Seat

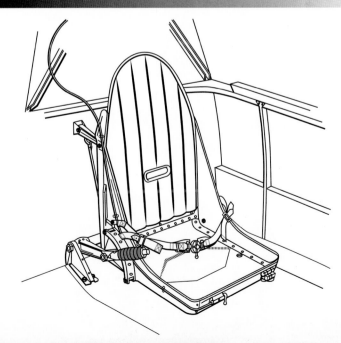

▸ Firefly FR.5 WB281 on a test flight in 'clean' configuration (no guns, drop tanks, or ASH nacelles fitted). The major difference between the FR.4 and FR.5 was that the latter could be converted to the day, night, or anti-submarine role with only minor changes.

▾ Deck hands prepare to launch Firefly FR.5 VT395 from the flight deck. The catapult gear consisted of a shuttle set in the flight deck, with a strop passed around it. Each end of the strop was then attached to the tail-down launching hooks. A hold-back link, which sheared when the aircraft was launched, was fixed near the tail. On this aircraft a glare shield has been fitted above the exhaust manifolds.

on strength, and it was decided to try them against the intruders. During October 1944 a number of these Fireflies were based temporarily at RAF Coltishall in Norfolk and were scrambled when radar detected the V-1-carrying He 111s coming in over the North Sea. Due to bad weather, poor ground radar directions, and odd equipment failures, there was only one occasion when a crew fired its guns blind into cloud after chasing a plot on their own ASH radar. The effort did, however, give crews experience of operating the Firefly in adverse operational conditions.

The first naval night-fighter unit was 1790 Squadron, which formed up in January 1945, followed by 1791 and 1792. None of these squadrons saw combat before the war ended. Training continued, and this led to the formation of 'Black Flights' whereby a flight of four Firefly night fighters were attached to day squadrons when embarked in carriers to provide night cover. This pioneering work eventually led to the modern all-weather two-seat fighters such as the de Havilland Sea Vixen and Blackburn Buccaneer.

One crew from 746 Squadron was embarked in escort carrier HMS *Searcher* for night deck landing trials and practice intruder interceptions. It was found that a Firefly NF.1 with full load had difficulty taking off safely in a deck wind of less than 25 knots. Subsequently, Rocket Assisted Take-Off (RATO) was recommended for operations from short decks..

Firefly T.1

This was a private project by Fairey to provide the FAA with an advanced dual-control trainer. The observer's cockpit was replaced by a second single pilot's cockpit. To achieve this, the fuselage top fairing was cut away from the decking at frame ten and replaced by a new structure designed to be attached to the top longerons and faired into the rear fuselage (▸▸ 27)

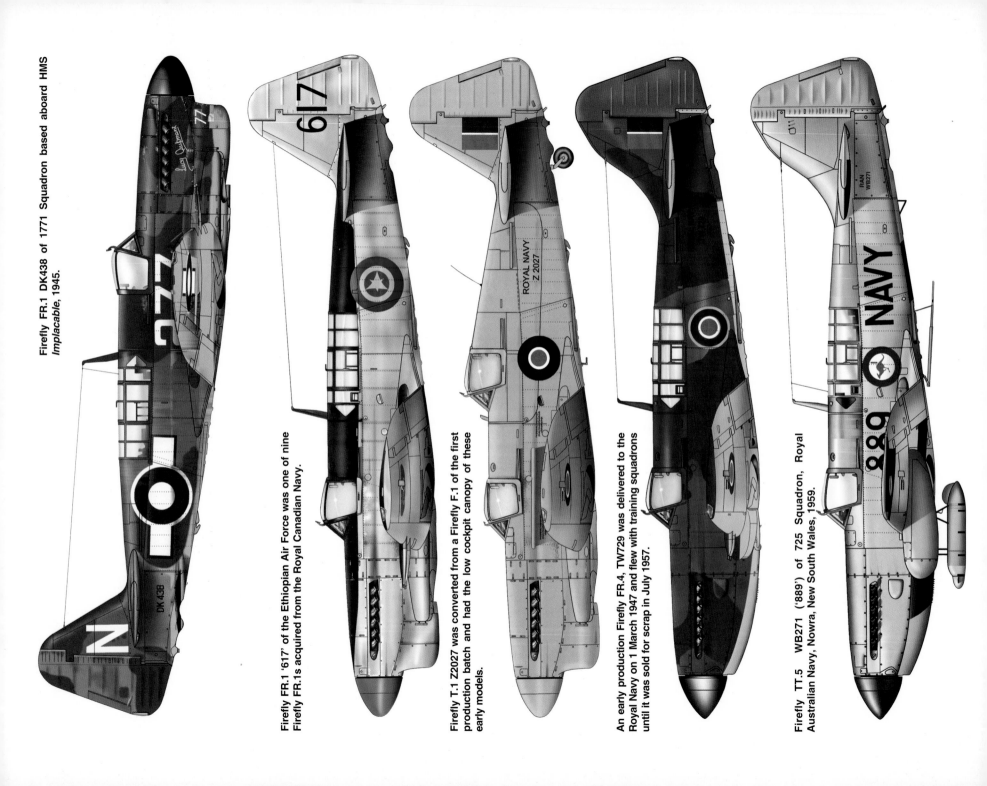

Firefly FR.1 DK438 of 1771 Squadron based aboard HMS *Implacable*, 1945.

Firefly FR.1 '617' of the Ethiopian Air Force was one of nine Firefly FR.1s acquired from the Royal Canadian Navy.

Firefly T.1 Z2027 was converted from a Firefly F.1 of the first production batch and had the low cockpit canopy of these early models.

An early production Firefly FR.4, TW729 was delivered to the Royal Navy on 1 March 1947 and flew with training squadrons until it was sold for scrap in July 1957.

Firefly TT.5 WB271 ('889') of 725 Squadron, Royal Australian Navy, Nowra, New South Wales, 1959.

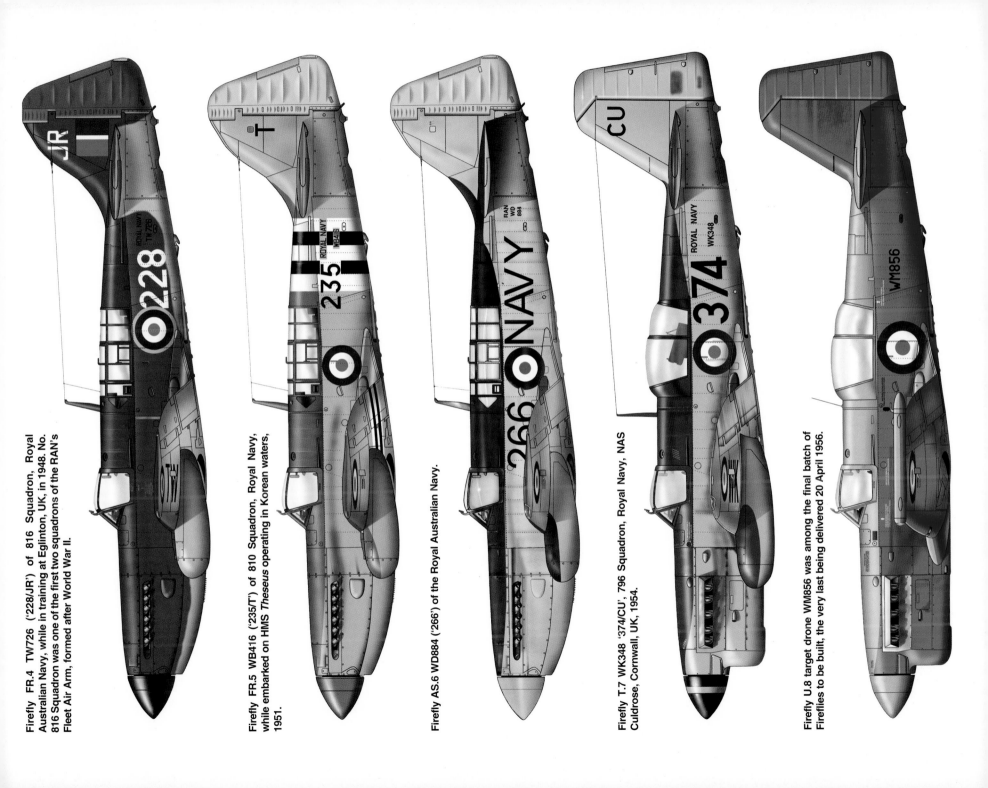

Firefly FR.4 TW726 ('228/JR') of 816 Squadron, Royal Australian Navy, while in training at Eglinton, UK, in 1948. No. 816 Squadron was one of the first two squadrons of the RAN's Fleet Air Arm, formed after World War II.

Firefly FR.5 WB416 ('235/T') of 810 Squadron, Royal Navy, while embarked on HMS *Theseus* operating in Korean waters, 1951.

Firefly AS.6 WD884 ('266') of the Royal Australian Navy.

Firefly T.7 WK348 '374/CU', 796 Squadron, Royal Navy, NAS Culdrose, Cornwall, UK, 1954.

Firefly U.8 target drone WM856 was among the final batch of Fireflies to be built, the very last being delivered 20 April 1956.

just forward of the fin root. The fuselage had to be widened slightly at the new cockpit location with a new turtleback and side fairings fitted. The new rear cockpit unit was raised by twelve inches so the instructor could have a better view.

The T.1s were not built new in the factory. When F.1/FR.1 aircraft came into the factory for repair, some would be allocated to the trainer conversion program, which entailed the fitting of the new rear cockpit and incorporation of all the latest modifications, including the later Griffon XII engine. One problem was that there wasn't enough room to run the dual throttle and propeller controls from the front to rear cockpits inside the fuselage, so they had to be housed in an external fairing on each side of the fuselage below and between the two cockpits. Some conversions were of the early F.1s with the low windshield and canopy while others were conversions of FR.1s with the raised windshield and canopy. This meant that T.1s could appear with different windshields and canopies.

The T.1 was not used for weapon training, although six were later converted by fitting one 20 mm cannon in each wing. Two Firefly 1s, Z2033 and MB750, served as trainer prototypes, followed by thirty-four conversions. After trials as a mock-up trainer, Z2033 was converted into a TT.1 target-tower and later sold to Sweden as SE-BRD. Prototype T.1 MB750 was later converted to T.2 standard and sold to the Royal Thai Navy.

Performance of the Firefly trainers was slightly better than the FR.1 due to the removal of operational equipment.

Firefly TT.1

War-surplus Fireflies proved to be an ideal aircraft for the target-towing role. During and up to the end of the war this task had been fulfilled by biplanes or monoplanes such as the Miles Martinet. In 1945, the British Admiralty indicated to the industry that they had a requirement for over ninety target-towing aircraft. No offers came from the aircraft industry, but in 1947 Svensk Flygjanst, a Swedish civil company providing target-towing facilities to the Swedish forces, expressed a need for more modern aircraft. Svensk asked Fairey Aviation about converting surplus Firefly 1s, and Fairey agreed to modify enough for the Swedes' requirements, buying the Fireflies back from the Admiralty. The factory installation comprised fitting a windlass arm just forward of the operator's cockpit on the port side. Attached to this was a standard Type 'B' Mark 2B cable winch, driven by a small propeller, which allowed target retraction when the firing detail was over. The windlass propeller could be rotated into a horizontal position to reduce drag when not in use.

In the roomy rear cockpit, a seat for the winch operator was fixed on the starboard side, but this could be raised out of the way when operating. This seat had a backrest with safety harness attached to the rear decking. When the operator was working, an additional harness anchorage point allowed him to move around. To facilitate viewing of the drogue streaming and recovery, a small windshield was mounted just forward of the rear canopy. Targets were stowed in a compartment just aft of the rear cockpit with a hinged door to the loading hatch below. To prevent fouling of control surfaces, external cable guards were fitted under the fuselage and around the tail unit. The operator had a foot-operated cable-cutter to cut the drogue target loose when required.

Recommended speed with a target trailed was 185 knots at sea level, although target tow missions were flown mostly at 215 to 235 knots, with a maximum of 260 knots. Svensk Flygtjanst AB eventually bought nineteen Firefly TT.1s and operated them successfully between 1948 and 1964. In 1951 the Royal Danish Air Force ordered two Firefly TT.1s and the following year acquired four Firefly 1s from the Royal Canadian Navy under the (▶ 28)

▲ Parked right at the extremity of the flight deck, this Firefly FR.5 is armed with two tiers of 3-inch rocket projectiles. Bomb carriers are also fitted but not loaded. The spinner and propeller have taken on a matt finish due to operating in the salt-laden atmosphere.

▼ Just about to grab the wire on HMS *Ocean* in 1949 is Firefly FR.5 VT462 ('200/O') of 812 Squadron. A squadron badge has been painted on the engine cowling.

▲ Firefly AS.5 WB428 ('208/FD'), seen at Ford NAS in 1954, shows the fitting of RATO gear. Code styles varied from unit to unit, and the fin code in this case reflects the unit's assigned station. The last two digits of the code number are painted on the landing gear door.

▼ A pilot shows off the attractive lines of Firefly AS.5 VT406 and the postwar camouflage scheme. The fuselage line sweeps back just onto the fin. The ASH radome on the starboard wing was not painted, as paint affected the operation of the radar. (Flight)

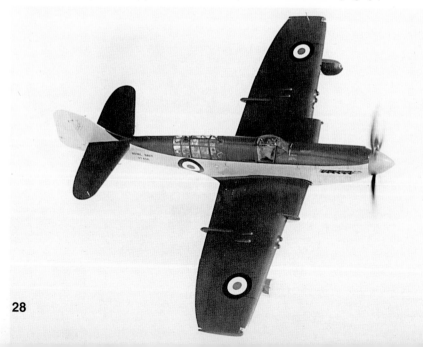

Mutual Aid Military Assistance Program. These were converted into TT.1s by the RDAF workshops at Vaerlose using conversion kits supplied by Fairey Aviation. The Indian Navy bought five Firefly TT.1s which were delivered in 1954. The British Admiralty did not order any.

Firefly NF. 2

The Admiralty interest in the Firefly as a night-fighter led to orders of 328, and that was before it had flown. All the radio and radar equipment was installed in the rear cockpit. This made the aircraft tail-heavy, so a 15-inch (38.1 cm) section was inserted in the fuselage between the engine bulkhead and the pilot's cockpit to bring the aircraft's center of gravity forward. Radar scanners were mounted in radomes on the wing, inboard between the cannon and fuselage. The first Firefly NF.2, Z1831/G (the 'G' indicated that the aircraft was on the secret list and had to have a guard at all times), went to Boscombe Down for trials in March 1943. Longitudinal stability was below the standard required, as the longer forward fuselage adversely affected its deck-landing capability. Synchronization of the radar scanners on the wings was also difficult. All these issues plus other minor problems led to the abandonment of the project in June 1944 after thirty-seven aircraft had been built. Some of these were converted to FR.1s before they left the factory, but a few NF.2s were retained for air interception trials from shore bases. Work went ahead to convert FR.1s on the assembly line to NF.1s.

Firefly T.2

The Firefly T.2 was a T.1 further modified as a tactical weapons trainer with gyro gunsights in both cockpits and one Hispano 20 mm cannon in each wing. It was cleared to carry 500-pound bombs, practice bombs, flares, markers, smoke floats, and mines. Some fifty-four conversions were carried out at Fairey Aviation's Stockport factory.

Firefly F.3

In February 1942, during a Firefly progress meeting at the Air Ministry, the idea of a single-seat version of the Firefly with the more powerful Rolls-Royce 1,980 hp Griffon 61 was raised. The Admiralty were not interested, saying that the Firefly's potential lay in its two-seat strike role. The Admiralty, however, did like the idea of the more powerful engine and in October that year informed the Air Ministry and Fairey that they would be ordering two hundred Firefly F.3 aircraft to be built as night-fighters. The tenth Firefly F.1 on the production line, Z1835, was earmarked as a trials aircraft for the Griffon 61. It was delivered to the Rolls-Royce Flight Test Establishment at Hucknall in Nottinghamshire on 24 May 1943, where it underwent fuel consumption and endurance trials. As this was an early production aircraft, it still had the low windshield and unfaired cannon. It also had been fitted with a new type of exhaust baffle.

Z1835 flew to Boscombe Down on 22 July for initial service handling trials, and the results were not good. There was high drag from the new engine installation. With flaps and landing gear down, there was longitudinal instability which also reduced the effectiveness of the elevator at low speeds. Directional control characteristics were poor, and it wanted to 'snake' in the climb. The rudder tended to overbalance to port, and when the aircraft was in a dive, yawing caused violent sideslips. The top speed of 300 knots at 18,300 feet was disappointing, as standard Firefly 1s at that height could already do 270 to 280 knots. With aerodynamic improvements due on the production line these speeds were expected to climb slightly, so the F.3 was not going to offer significantly better performance. At a meeting on 16 December 1944, the Firefly

F.3 program was officially terminated. The contracts were cancelled, and eventually Z1835 was converted into one of the Firefly FR.4 prototypes.

Firefly T.3

With the availability of both the Firefly T.1 and T.2, operational flight training for naval pilots was not a problem, but in the late 1940's there was nothing suitable to train observers for aerial combat. Consequently, the Admiralty asked Fairey if they could convert a number of Fireflies to do the job. The result was the Firefly T.Mk.3, a quick conversion of a standard Firefly FR.1. The cockpits remained the same, but special detection equipment was installed in the rear one to train observers in the role of anti-submarine warfare. The deck arrester hook and all armament were deleted and other minor changes made. The rear cockpit only allowed one observer to be trained at a time, but this was better than nothing! Some fifty conversions were made by Fairey engineers between 1949 and 1951 working at naval maintenance yards.

Firefly FR.4

The failure of the Firefly F.3 led to some re-thinking and design changes. The more powerful 2,330 hp Rolls-Royce Griffon 72 engine replaced the Griffon 61 and drove a four-bladed Rotol propeller. Leading edge radiators were introduced with two short-barrel Hispano Mk.V 20 mm cannon installed in each wing. The wing tips were cropped to give a better rate of roll. An ASH radome under the port wing was counterbalanced by a fuel tank under the starboard wing. Initially the original Mk.1 fin and rudder were used, but aerodynamic trials dictated a change in profile. Four prototypes (Z1835, Z2118, MB649, and PP4820), all converted Mk.1s, were used, with the first, Z2118, flying on 25 May, 1945. It retained the elliptical wings and original tail assembly of the Mk.1, but these were changed later that year to the new profile. The first few F.4s were F.1s converted on the production line, but by then the 2,245 hp Griffon 74 had replaced the Griffon 72 with the first production Firefly FR.4, TW722, being delivered to the FAA in September 1946. Minor problems delayed its introduction, but to get it into use it was initially cleared on 12 February 1947 for shore-based operations with spinning and aerobatics prohibited and diving speed limited to 370 knots. These restrictions were lifted by mid-1947.

No.825 Squadron, at that time loaned to the Royal Canadian Navy (RCN), was the first to receive the new Firefly FR.4 in August 1947, followed by 810 Squadron in October, with 812 and 814 Squadrons re-equipping with the FR.4 early in 1948. Second-line squadrons operating the FR.4 for training included 703, 727, 767, 778, 781, and 799 Squadrons. Pilots found the FR.4 an overall improvement over the Mk.1s — it was faster and had a higher rate of roll due to its clipped wings.

The FR.4 was only in use with front-line squadrons for a relatively short period, and by late 1950 the majority of FR.4s had been replaced by the FR.5. Firefly FR.4 TW695 was flight tested with contra-rotating propellers, but any advantages they may have given were not considered worth adopting and the idea was shelved. Some Firefly FR.4s were transferred to Commonwealth naval air arms and/or converted to the target-towing role.

Firefly TT.4

Although the Admiralty had not been interested in a Firefly TT.1 conversion, they became quite enthusiastic when they learned that Fairey was offering a simple design change to the Firefly 4 and 5 to provide a target-towing capability. The actual changes were quite small, as most of them were to the outside of the aircraft. A Type 'G' Mk 3 winch and Type (➡ 33)

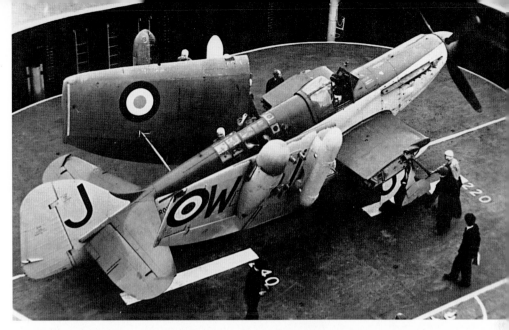

▲ A Firefly AS.6 is brought up to the flight deck on HMS *Eagle*'s lift. The small deck area needed by the Firefly when its wings were folded is apparent.

▼ Firefly AS.6 aircraft of 812 and 814 Squadrons, on the flight deck of HMS *Eagle* in 1953, are readied for a 3-inch rocket firing exercise. A full load of rocket projectiles is carried, eight on each side. Anti-glare shields are fitted above the exhaust manifolds for night flying. On the aft flight deck are Sea Hornet NF.21s of 809 Squadron, more Fireflies, and two Douglas AEW.1 (AD-4W) Skyraiders, forty of which were passed to the FAA under the MDAP (Mutual Defense Assistance Program).

▾ The fine lines of the Firefly AS.6 are shown in this picture of WD917 ('203/FD') when in service with 1840 Squadron, an anti-submarine Royal Navy Volunteer Reserve (RNVR) air unit, at NAS Ford in 1951. Although the AS.6 had no guns, it could still pack a powerful punch with its rocket projectiles and bomb carriers. This aircraft was sold for scrap in July 1956. (Flight)

▴ A Firefly AS.6 WD838 about to be launched from the flight deck of HMAS *Sydney*. The Fairey-Youngman flaps are set to the take-off position. This aircraft flew with the Royal Australian Navy for eight years before being sold to a private owner. (RAN)

▴ VT406 was built as an FR.5 in 1948 and used by 703 Squadron. After conversion to AS.6 standard, it was used by 737, 826, and 1844 RNVR Squadrons before being scrapped in 1956. It is seen here as '278/R' of 826 Squadron when operating from HMS *Glory*. It may have had an accident or engine change at some point, as indicated by the unpainted and dirty engine cowling panels.

▾ Firefly AS.6 WH628 with (in background) WJ104, both of 1840 RNVR Squadron when based at Ford in 1951-52. This unit, operating in the anti-submarine role, was staffed by full-time officers and ratings but augmented by part-time reserve crews.

The prototype Firefly AS.7 MB757 after a new canopy had been fitted over the rear cockpit. The arrestor hook has been retained, and the aircraft still has the Mk.4 style tail. The more bulbous nose profile is due to installation of a Griffon 57 engine. Rear nacelle mountings are below the wing ready to receive radar equipment.

Firefly AS.7 WJ200 shows the final form of this variant, with revised fin and rudder, different exhaust baffles, and deleted tail hook. All Mk.7s were the same. Sonobuoy racks are mounted below the wings.

▲ All the features of the Firefly T.7 are shown in this picture of WJ149 — the revised wing, new engine exhaust system, rear bubble cockpit canopy, longer horizontal stabilizer, and taller fin and rudder. (Flight)

▼ Firefly T.7 WK348 '374/CU' out on a training detail during 1954 while serving with 796 Squadron based at NAS Culdrose in Cornwall. Unless its airframe was cleaned regularly, the Firefly's appearance was marred by exhaust stains.

▲ An underside view of the Firefly T.7 WK368 '337/GN' shows some similarity to its predecessor, the Firefly 1. The flaps are at CRUISE setting, allowing the pilot to break sharply away from the photographic aircraft. (Flight)

▼ Firefly T.7s WK368 ('337/GN'), WJ188 ('322/GN'), and WJ165 ('329/GN') of 719 Squadron, based at NAS Eglinton, Northern Ireland, practice formation flying with other units for a review of the fleet by Her Majesty Queen Elizabeth II in 1953. (Flight)

'B' Mk 2 exchanger unit plus associated equipment were contained in a bomb-shaped pod mounted beneath the center section. A small two-blade wooden propeller located at the front of the pod drove the winch; the propeller could be fully feathered when not in use. For aerodynamic reasons a small fin was added to the rear of the container. The wing 20 mm cannon and engine mounting ballast were removed, as was the ASH radar, although the radome and fuel tank were retained. The beauty of this modification was that, as the Firefly 4, 5, and 6 were all similar, it could be fitted to any of them to convert them for the target-towing role.

The Admiralty ordered twenty-eight Firefly FR.4s from their own stocks to be modified into TT.4s. The Indian Navy also ordered five such conversions to add to the five TT.1s ordered earlier. All the conversions were ex-FAA aircraft. The Dutch and Australian Navies carried out their own conversions using kits provided by Fairey Aviation.

Firefly NF.4

When converted to the night-fighter role, which included radio interception, the Firefly FR.4 was redesignated Firefly NF.4. The actual changes were small and did not affect the appearance or performance of the aircraft.

Firefly FR.5

The incorporation of all the experience gained in operating the Firefly FR.4 with later, more up-to-date equipment led to the multi-role Firefly FR.5, probably the most successful of all the Firefly variants built. Changes included the fitting of radome vibration dampers to give better radar reception and the introduction of powered wing-folding. Hydraulic wing-folding jacks, controlled by a three-gate lever in the pilot's cockpit, were fitted into the center section. Deliveries to front-line squadrons began in January 1948 and continued until May 1950. Of the 444 ordered, 338 were built for the Royal Navy, some were cancelled, and the last sixteen were converted into the Firefly AS.6.

The first units to fly the FR.5 were the Service Trials squadrons, Nos. 778 and 782, who started receiving them in May 1948. The first front-line unit to receive the FR.5 was 812 Squadron, which took them aboard the carrier HMS *Glory* in July 1948 for a shake-down cruise in the Mediterranean. In September 1948 812 Squadron returned to the United Kingdom to pick up some updated FR.5s and then embarked in *Glory* as part of the 13th CAG (Carrier Air Group). They were in far eastern waters when the Korean War broke out and were quickly in action, staying until May 1952. No. 814 Squadron exchanged its FR.4s for FR.5s in 1949 and had a brief tour embarked in the carrier HMS *Vengeance* in the Mediterranean, changing to the Firefly AS.6 in November 1950. Between June and December 1949, when they had problems with their Supermarine Seafires, No. 804 Squadron also flew the FR.5. On 17 October 1949, 810 Squadron accepted Firefly AS.5s as part of the 17th CAG, but these were exchanged for FR.5s when the squadron was posted to the Korean War zone. After completing a series of strikes against Korean targets, the squadron moved back to the U.K. where it spent most of 1951 afloat in carriers HMS *Glory*, HMS *Ocean*, and HMS *Theseus* before returning to *Ocean* for another round of strikes over Korea. July 1951 saw 820 Squadron accepting AS.5s, but these were changed for the AS.6 in December 1951. A Firefly AS.6 unit, 821 Squadron, changed to the FR.5 and operated in Korea until May 1953. Another Firefly unit operating in Korea was 825 Squadron, embarked in *Ocean* as part of the 17th CAG with 802's Sea Furies, and these continued to carry out strikes against the enemy. With the armistice the Firefly squadrons were withdrawn to the U.K., leaving the Royal Australian Navy's Fireflies and Sea Furies aboard HMAS *Sydney* to provide aerial reconnaissance and patrols.
(▸ 34)

▲ The highly colorful Firefly U.8 target drone. WM856 displays upper surfaces of fluorescent yellow and lower surfaces of fluorescent red in accordance with 'Pattern 2,' which specified that the upper surface color could not exceed one quarter of the depth of the fuselage. The fin and rudder were considered to be undersurfaces. Spinners were yellow. Roundels are standard, and the serial number is black.

▼ Firefly U.8 WM810 undergoing maintenance at Llanbedr, the base of the ministry guided weapons unit. The letter 'A,' barely visible on the fin, was in yellow.

▲ Two Firefly U.9s of 728B Squadron based at Hal Far, Malta. '591' is WB257, the first U.9; converted by Fairey during 1955-56, it was shot down by a missile off Malta on 25 May 1960. Both aircraft have their camera pods removed. The wing tanks are red except for the area under the leading edge of the wing, which was yellow, and antiglare black over half the nose section. Both have white upper surfaces and codes. '591' has a yellow spinner, '596' a white spinner.

Firefly NF.5

Like the FR.4s, the FR.5s could be converted to the night-fighter role and when operating in this mode were known as NF.5s. They were fitted with ARI 5664, which gave warning when another aircraft approached from the rear. A warning bell sounded behind the pilot, and there was also a warning light on the pilot's starboard cockpit coaming. Also fitted was an ARI 5284 radio altimeter.

Firefly AS.5

This was an FR.5 used in the anti-submarine role. An ARI 5284 radio altimeter was fitted. When used in the anti-submarine role the aircraft was also fitted with an ARI 5286 sonobuoy installation, controlled from the observer's cockpit. The sonobuoy aerial in the observer's cockpit had to be retracted before landing. Stores carried included twelve sonobuoys and two depth charges.

Firefly T.5

The Firefly T.5 was a Royal Australian Navy conversion of the Firefly FR.5 using drawings and conversion kits provided by Fairey Aviation in the U.K. The conversion was similar to the one carried out in the U.K. on the Firefly 1 to create the T.1 and T.2 trainers with a raised rear cockpit. Some local redesign was necessary, and this was done by Fairey Aviation Co. of Australia Pty.,

a subsidiary of the main company in the U.K. As on the Firefly 1 an external fairing below the pilot's cockpit had to be installed for the throttle and propeller control runs. One 20 mm cannon was retained in each wing for weapon training. Only four conversions were done, on VT440, VT502, VX373, and VX375, to provide advanced training and conversion for pilots who were moving on to the Firefly 5.

Firefly TT.5

Two Firefly 5s of the Royal Australian Navy, WB251 and VX388, were converted to provide naval target-towing capability. These were straight conversions, as for the Firefly TT.4, entailing the fitting of a Type 'G' Mk.3 winch under the forward fuselage.

Firefly AS.6

Concern about submarine detection in the post-war era led to the need for carrier-borne aircraft to carry out this duty. The Firefly AS.5 was capable of limited anti-submarine operations but required a dedicated, third crew member. The Admiralty also was asking Fairey if the Firefly AS.5 could carry both American and British sonobuoys. To accommodate these and other internal detection gear, some re-design was necessary, the resulting changes sufficient to warrant a new designation, Firefly AS.6. Modifications included a GM4B compass, a Type 62 radio aerial, longer-stroke landing gear oleo struts, a re-designed deck hook damper, and new snap gear. It was felt that in the anti-submarine role defensive armament was not required, so the four 20 mm cannon were deleted. Standard 45- and 90-gallon drop tanks could still be carried and jettisoned, while the fuel cell on the port wing and the ASH radome on the starboard wing, which were part of the airframe, were retained. Hard points on each wing allowed the carriage of eight 3-inch rocket projectiles in two tiers of four between the landing gear leg and the outer tanks. These same points allowed the carriage of sonobuoys and other naval stores such as depth charges and mines. The first AS.6 was WB423, a modified AS.5, but the first true AS.6 built on the production line was WB505, which flew on 23 March 1949. Fairey was informed that 131 Firefly AS.5s were to be converted to AS.6 and was requested to transfer the first nineteen, WB422 through WB440, to their Stockport factory where the work was to be carried out. In fact only sixteen were converted before proper AS.6 production got under way, with 133 eventually built.

No 814 Squadron became the first to receive the Firefly AS.6 in January 1951. Along with 809 Squadron's Sea Hornets, it formed the 7th Night Air Group which, embarked in HMS *Vengeance*, became the FAA's first all-weather unit. In September 814 Squadron joined the 15th CAG aboard HMS *Theseus*, eventually transferring to HMS *Eagle*. Other front-line squadrons operating the AS.6 included 812, 816, 817, 820, 821, 824, 826, and 851 Squadrons and reserve squadrons 1830, 1840, 1841, and 1844. Second-line units using the AS.6 were 703, 703A, 719, 723, 724, 737, 737X, 744, 751, 767, 771, 782, and 796 Squadrons The continuous modification and development of anti-submarine warfare equipment gradually overtook the capabilities of a single operator, and the Firefly AS.6 was withdrawn at the end of 1955.

Firefly TT.6

Four Firefly AS.6 aircraft, WB518, WD828, WD840, and WD901, were converted by the Royal Australian Navy for target-towing duties. These were straight conversions as done on the Firefly TT.4 and TT.5 using the Type 'G' Mk.3 winch.

Firefly AS/T.7

A three-seat anti-submarine version of the Firefly, the AS.7, proved to be a disaster. It was intended to be used as an interim substitute for the new three-seat Fairey Gannet dedicated anti-submarine aircraft, development of which was behind schedule. The design changes necessary to meet Admiralty requirements resulted in a completely different airplane. An old Mk.1, MB757, was set aside for conversion to the new AS.7 prototype. The powerplant was to be a 1,960-hp Rolls-Royce Griffon 57 but with an annular chin radiator installation similar to the Firefly 1 instead of the leading edge radiators of later variants. The pilot's cockpit was a standard Firefly cockpit, but the wings were semi-elliptical, similar to the Mk.1, with the 20 mm guns deleted. The radomes for the new ASV-19A radar were a different size from those of the older ASH installation, so they had to be moved to the outer wing. As the rear cockpit now had to accommodate two operators and all their equipment, a bulged rear canopy was adopted to give the operators a better view, including downward, for sonobuoy operations. The horizontal stabilizer was a standard Mk.6 layout.

Test flights and further Admiralty changes resulted in comprehensive design modifications. The pilot's cockpit had to be raised twelve inches and redesigned to new SBAC (Society of British Aircraft Constructors) standards. The wing leading edge needed a fillet near the fuselage. Handling trials showed instability with the standard horizontal stabilizer, so this was increased in span from fourteen to eighteen feet. Longitudinal directional stability was poor, and this led to a taller and more angular fin and rudder. Improvements to the landing gear were also required.

Fairey and Boscombe Down test pilots found the performance of the Firefly AS.7 poorer than that of the Firefly AS.6; low-speed handling, critical for carrier operations, was especially troublesome. The changes had put more induced drag on the airframe, and service pilots declared the AS.7 unsafe for carrier operations. But the Admiralty wanted their three-seat anti-submarine aircraft and placed order after order until a total of 337 aircraft had been requested. Eventually the Firefly AS.7 program was cut back to 151 aircraft, with 110 built at the Hayes factory and forty-one at Stockport, but they were to be used only in a training role ashore as the T.7. They entered service from 1953 onwards and served with 719, 750, 765, 796, and 1840 Squadrons before being gradually replaced by the Gannet in 1955/56.

Firefly T.7D

This designation was applied to two Firefly T.7 aircraft, WJ216 and WJ217, which were to join the target drone program but were completed as drone pilot test bed aircraft.

Firefly U.7

One Firefly T.7 was used to test equipment for the proposed Firefly U.8 target drone but was later converted to full U.8 status.

Firefly T.8

Six Firefly T.7s, WJ147, WJ149, WJ150, WJ151, WJ152, and WJ153, were used as trials aircraft or chase machines in the early days of the target-drone program. All were later converted to full U.8 standard.

(▸ 36)

▲ The nearest Firefly U.9, '590,' is pilotless and is being guided by the rear machine, '595,' which has a crew. Both are from 728B Squadron and were photographed on 8 July 1958 near Malta. The U.9 was fitted with a longer arrestor hook taken from Hawker Sea Hawk naval stocks because the drone, when being returned to base, had to be flown on to the runway in a 'wheel' landing, and not a three-point landing. The longer hook increased the likelihood of the Firefly's catching an arrestor cable.

▼ Firefly U.9 VT487 '590' seen from the shepherd aircraft near Malta on 8 July 1958. VT487 was delivered to the FAA in September 1948 and joined 737 Squadron. It was transferred to 821 Squadron and flew operations over Korea during 1952-53, with both 821 and 810 Squadrons. After returning to the U.K. it re-joined 737 Squadron before being converted to drone status by Fairey Aviation in 1956-57. It joined 728B Squadron 3 February 1958.

▲ Firefly Trainer F.1 after conversion from FR.1 MB750. It was silver overall with a black upper fuselage surface. The single cannon in each wing reflects the advanced trainer concept Fairey wanted to sell to the Admiralty. The arrestor hook is still fitted. Both cockpits exhibit the raised windshield and higher hood. Anti-spin strakes are fitted to the top of the fin.

Firefly U.8

The Firefly U.8 was a pilotless target drone for guided weapons development. A total of forty were produced, six from conversions of Firefly T.7s and thirty-four from new production. The pilot's cockpit was identical to that of the T.7 but with all unnecessary equipment removed. Extraneous equipment also was removed from the observer's cockpit, and a radio-controlled Mk.8 Type H automatic pilot, which allowed control from the ground, was installed. The Rotol four-blade propeller was locked at 2600 rpm for pilotless flight. Recording cameras were fitted in wing-tip pods. The first Firefly U.8 conversion flew on 27 November 1953.

The majority of the U.8s were used by the Royal Aircraft Establishment (RAE) at the ministry drone airfield at Llanbedr in Wales, although radio control of pilotless aircraft was done from either Llanbedr or Aberporth, a coastal station. The first unmanned flight from Llanbedr was in February 1954. Progressive development continued during 1954 and early 1955, and it was 29 September 1955 when the first Firefly U.8 drone, WM886, was successfully shot down by an air-launched missile from a De Havilland Venom jet fighter.

Radio control during the early days was quite primitive, with test flights being done using a 'shepherd' aircraft flying alongside with a controller in the rear cockpit. Two controllers standing on either side of the runway were required to land the aircraft, not so easy with a tail-dragger! With experience operations and equipment improved, even if the end result was the destruction of the Firefly.

In November 1959, the Canadian carrier HMCS *Bonaventure* was taking part in North Atlantic Treaty organization (NATO) exercises around the coasts of Europe. Six McDonnell F2H-3

Banshee jet fighters of 870 Squadron were detached ashore to Llanbedr and, armed with AIM-9 Sidewinder missiles, shot down five Firefly drones over the Aberporth ranges. Many of those that were not shot down ended their days providing spares before consigned to the scrap yard.

Firefly U.9

With the success of the drone program, the Ministry of Supply (MoS), which had replaced the wartime MAP, placed an order for a further forty drone aircraft. However, by then all the stocks of production Firefly 7s and 8s had been used up in converting them to U.8s. Consequently, Fairey offered to convert forty surplus Firefly FR.5s. Designated Firefly U.9, the conversion differed somewhat from the U.8 due to the different aerodynamic characteristics of the FR.5 airframe, which required changes to the automatic control system. Firefly FR.5 WB416 was the first U.9 test aircraft with the first real conversion flying from Ringway on 13 December 1956. Most of the forty U.9s were used by No.728B Squadron of the FAA, initially as targets for Armstrong Siddeley Seaslug ship-to-air missiles fired from the new missile ship HMS *Girdleness*. The squadron was established on 13 January 1958 at the FAA airfield Stretton, not far from the Fairey flight test airfield at Ringway. It later moved to the naval base at Hal Far, Malta to provide drone aircraft for the Royal Navy. Eventually 728B Squadron operated thirty-three Firefly U.9s. The last, WB391, was shot down by the guns of HMS *Duchess* on 27 November 1961, ending the saga of the Firefly.

Fireflies in Combat

The Firefly more than proved its worth in combat. On 17 July 1944 Firefly 1s of 1770 Squadron, embarked in HMS *Indefatigable*, flew flak suppression sorties using rockets and 20 mm cannon against more than fifty flak sites when supporting naval air attacks on the German battleship *Tirpitz*. More strikes were made against *Tirpitz* during August, when more Fireflies were lost in action. The second Firefly unit, 1771 Squadron, embarked in HMS *Implacable*, attacked German shipping, enemy airfields in Norway, and seaplane bases and other targets along the Norwegian coast, resulting in the destruction of numerous ships and aircraft. None of the Fireflies saw air-to-air combat.

Because of their striking power, the Firefly squadrons joined the projected British Pacific Fleet (BPF) at Ceylon (now Sri Lanka) and sailed for the Far East, where they were to join the American Pacific Fleet for attacks on Japanese-held islands in the push to Japan. On the way, Rear Admiral Vian carried out a number of attacks on Japanese oil refineries in Sumatra. On 4 January 1945, 1770 Squadron carried out attacks on oil refineries at Pangkalan Brandon as part of a 400-aircraft strike. Japanese fighters appeared, and Lt. Levitt opened the score for the squadron when he shot down a Nakajima Ki.43 *Hayabusa* ('Oscar'). On 24 January. 1770 Squadron attacked Pladjoe refinery, where two more Japanese fighters fell to the guns of the Fireflies. During a raid on the refinery at Songi Gerong near Palembang, three more Oscars were shot down by 1770's Fireflies.

The BPF, known as Task Force 57, was wanted by General MacArthur and Admiral Nimitz but was eventually absorbed into Admiral Spruance's 5th Fleet for the proposed attack against Okinawa. The BPF was tasked with attacking any enemy positions in the Sakishima Gunto group of islands to prevent any intervention by Japanese units based there, or to prevent reinforcements flying in once the action started. During the next few months. the Fireflies continually attacked and destroyed many airfields, aircraft on the airfields, numerous radar stations, and various shipping, some aircraft and crews being lost to flak. (▶ 39)

▲ The student pilot's cockpit of a Firefly T.1 trainer. The lever on the left cockpit wall is the flap selector. The bucket seat was designed to take the standard British naval seat parachute and emergency pack. Test instrumentation has been fitted to this aircraft in place of the Mk.4E gyro gunsight.

▲ The rear (instructor's) cockpit of a Firefly T.2 trainer. The new cockpit, raised 12 inches to give the instructor a better view, had fewer instruments than the front (student's) cockpit. A Mk.4E gyro gunsight was fitted to both cockpits. Catapult take-offs and arrested landings on a carrier were the same as for a Firefly FR.1.

▶ Firefly Trainer T.1 Z2027 seen in overall yellow in 1948. Z2027 had originally been delivered to the FAA in June 1944, and after service with 790 Squadron went to Fairey's factory for conversion to a trainer. As a trainer it served with 810, 771, and 767 Squadrons before suffering an engine failure and belly landing in March 1954.

◀ Later marks of Firefly could also be converted for the training role, such as VX373, a Firefly T.5 in use with the Royal Australian Navy. Like some of the Firefly T.1 or T.2 trainers, the front cockpit windshield has been lowered to give the instructor in the rear cockpit a better view. The fuselage fairing below the front cockpit contained the aft cockpit's throttle and mixture control cables, which could not be fitted within the fuselage. One cannon was retained in each wing.

On 12 April 1945 the Fireflies of 1770 Squadron were split up, some to provide combat air patrol duty over the fleet, while others attacked shipping and harbor installations. Two crews were detailed to escort a US Navy Martin PBM-5 Mariner flying boat to pick up some ditched aircrews near the Sakashima Gunto islands. Over the island of Yonakumi Shima, the two Fireflies spotted five Mitsubishi Ki-51 'Sonia' dive bombers on their way to Okinawa. Breaking away from the PBM, Lt. Ward, with observer S/Lt. Stott, shot down two Sonias, as did S/Lt. Miller with S/Lt. Thomson. A fifth Sonia was seen diving away and smoking. The following day, Fireflies of 1770 Squadron destroyed a radar station at Yonakumi with rockets and then strafed small enemy boats. The whole fleet was saddened later that day to hear that President Roosevelt had passed away. May was very busy with strikes against airfields, storehouses, motor transport, barracks, oil and fuel storage depots, barges, shipping, and a new threat, suicide boats. On 24 May, the BPF sailed to Australia to replenish. Some 5,335 sorties had been flown by all types. Ninety-eight enemy aircraft had been destroyed in combat and more than that on the ground. The BPF had lost twenty-six aircraft to enemy action, forty-one aircrew losing their lives.

When the BPF returned to the battle zone after replenishment, 1770 Squadron had been replaced aboard *Indefatigable* by 1772 Squadron, with 1771 Squadron aboard *Implacable*. These squadrons were part of Task Force 111/2, formed under Rear Admiral E. J. B. Brind with orders to attack Truk in the Caroline Islands. After this mission, the Task Force joined up with the US Third Fleet and operations against enemy targets restarted on 17 July.

A typical day for the Firefly squadrons was 24 July 1945. On this date, 1771 Squadron attacked Japanese shipping in the Inland Sea near Nagoya while other Fireflies attacked a destroyer in Ono Bay. Out on an early morning strike, 1772 Squadron attacked the enemy airfield at Tokushima; that afternoon 1772 attacked the airfield at Takamatsu in Shikoku near Japan, losing one Firefly and its crew to flak. The weather that day was poor, but a force of six Avengers, two Corsairs, and two Fireflies from 1771 Squadron, armed with rockets, found the Japanese escort carrier *Kaiyo* and carried out a series of attacks which left the carrier on fire with a broken back. Throughout July and August, the Fleets kept up almost daily strikes against Japanese targets, which by now included the Japanese mainland. On 27 August, the Fireflies of 1772 Squadron were given a new task – location of Allied POW camps so that medical supplies could be dropped. On 2 September 1945, some of 1772's Fireflies flew over a POW camp at Yokkaichi during which a Boeing B-29 Superfortress of the USAAF arrived and dropped supplies. The war was over!

Malaya

Unrest in the Malayan peninsula began at the end of World War II. Chinese guerrilla forces, armed by the Allies, fought against the Japanese and after hostilities had no wish to return to British and other foreign rule. They started a series of attacks against property, plantations, and people. In 1948, 'Operation Firedog,' an emergency campaign against the terrorists, was launched. British air and ground forces carried out attacks which would continue until 1957 when Malaya became an independent nation. Whenever a British carrier was in Far Eastern waters, its CAG would operate strikes against terrorists using Fireflies and Sea Furies in support of ground forces. These strikes usually employed rockets, which were more effective at jungle targets, followed by strafing attacks. These missions provided realistic training for the CAGs, and when carriers were on their way to Korea during 1950-53, their Fireflies and Sea Furies continued to carry out strikes against Malayan terrorist strongholds, giving younger and inexperienced pilots valuable training for combat in Korea.

(▸ 42)

▲ Royal Australian Navy Firefly AS.6 WD884 ('266') showing the larger markings adopted by the RAN late in the life of their Fireflies. Colors followed the Royal Navy pattern, and like the Royal Navy, the RAN also eliminated the fin flash. Glare shields are installed above the engine exhausts. Crew names are listed below the windshield area. (RAN)

▼ Two Firefly TT.6 aircraft, WJ109 ('907/NW') and WB518 ('903/NW') of 851 Squadron RAN, prepare to depart Bankstown for their base at Nowra. Finish for target-towers was overall silver with black and yellow stripes on undersurfaces and spinners. By this time the Kangaroo had appeared in the center of the Australian roundel. 'NW' on the fin is the code for the naval base at Nowra. (RAN)

▲ Imperial Ethiopian Air Force Firefly FR.1s in their original two-tone colour scheme of light stone and brown with red spinners.

▲ Firefly FR.1 '617' of the Imperial Ethiopian Air Force at Asmara after being retired from active service. This was one of nine Firefly FR.1s acquired from the Royal Canadian Navy, with the markings of the latter still just visible after sitting in the hot sun for more than 20 years!

▼ Royal Canadian Navy Firefly AS.5 VH135 'BD•K' showing the same colors as used by the Royal Navy (Extra Dark Sea Gray upper surfaces and Sky lower surface) except for the smaller fuselage roundel with a maple leaf in the center. When delivered they had the standard Royal Navy roundel. The spinner was sky. (RCN)

▼ Three Firefly FR.1s of the Royal Netherlands Naval Air Service (MLD) fire rocket projectiles at terrorist targets in the Dutch East Indies. By this time the Netherlands' national marking had changed from a large orange triangle to a small orange circle within a larger trisected red, white, and blue circle. (Dutch Navy)

▲ 'Sharkmouth' Firefly FR.4 of the MLD (*Marine Luchtvaardienst* — Royal Netherlands Naval Air Service) at Biak, New Guinea in 1959-60. Its guns have been deleted for some reason, but four rocket rails under each wing still give it some punch. "KON. MARINE" is an abbreviation of "*Koninklijke Marine*," which is Dutch for "Royal Navy." (Dutch Navy)

▼ Firefly TT.4 INS119 of the Indian Navy. Indian Navy Fireflies were silver overall with black and yellow stripes on the undersurfaces, black spinners, and black lettering. Delivered in 1958, they were used by 550 Squadron at Cochin.

▲ All-yellow Firefly TT.1 '625' of the Royal Danish Air Force (RDAF) was converted from early Firefly F1 Z1842 in 1951 and still has the low pilot's windshield and canopy. RDAF Fireflies were delivered in Danish national markings with black serial numbers. The target-towing windlass can be seen in the horizontal transit position. (RDAF)

▼ This Swedish Firefly TT.1 SE-BRA was the first of Svensk Flygjanst AB's fleet of sixteen, although three others were bought from Denmark and broken up for use as spares. The wind deflector in front of the rear cockpit was deleted when the aircraft was used in Sweden.

▲ Firefly FR.1 '4Q' of 1770 Squadron gets airborne from HMS *Indefatigable* on 4 January 1945 for a strike against the Japanese-held oil refinery at Pangkalan Brandan. It carries eight 60-lb, 3-in rocket projectiles on Mk.1 rails bolted to a blast plate fastened under the wing with four hooks. A protective cover was fitted over the landing light on the port wing when rocket projectiles were carried. The flaps are in the take-off position. SEAC roundels were repeated on the upper wing and fuselage but in a larger size. A small 'Q' can just be discerned on the inner wing leading edge. (IWM)

▼ Flak-damaged Firefly FR.1 DV124 ('274/S') of 1770 Squadron is manhandled along the flight deck after returning successfully to HMS *Indefatigable* after a raid against Japanese targets. The revised SEAC markings consisted of one roundel on the port upper wing and one on the starboard lower wing. Fuselage side codes were changed from a numeral/letter to a three-digit code. (IWM)

Fireflies over Korea

Within five days of the North Korean push south to Seoul, the British carrier HMS *Triumph* and a small force of cruisers and destroyers were at action stations off the Korean coast. Aboard *Triumph* was the 13th CAG, consisting of 827 Squadron with twelve Firefly FR.1s and 800 Squadron with twelve Seafire F.47s. Tactical commander of Task Force 77, a British and American combined fleet, was US Navy Rear Admiral Hoskins carrying his flag in the American carrier USS *Valley Forge* (CV-45). On 3 July 1950, Fireflies and Seafires opened the offensive with attacks on Haeju airfield. Then followed a series of strikes against railway bridges and troop positions. To avoid misidentification by sailors and troops of United Nations forces, British aircraft had black and white stripes applied on their outer wings and rear fuselages, and British aircraft carriers had a Union Jack flag painted on the deck. During July, the Seafires provided CAP while Fireflies were used for coastal surveillance. On 16 August, a small force of North Korean coastal craft were detected in the Taedong estuary, and six Fireflies and six Seafires using rockets damaged a minesweeper, freighter, and other craft. In early September, the Fireflies and Seafires carried out a series of strikes against railway targets, destroying trains, rolling stock and three tunnels when rockets were fired into both entrances. The 13th CAG provided air cover along the coast for the Inchon landings, but by the time the carrier withdrew, they only had two serviceable Fireflies and one Seafire. Most of 827 Squadron's Fireflies had already seen service at the end of World War II, and maintenance and lack of spares had become problems.

HMS *Theseus,* with the 17th CAG embarked, arrived off the Korean coast to relieve *Triumph* in early October. On board were twelve Firefly FR.5s of 810 Squadron and twenty-one Sea Furies of 807 Squadron. Each carrier, British or American, usually carried out a patrol then withdrew to replenish while another carrier replaced it. *Theseus*'s first patrol was between 9 and 22 October 1950. Her squadrons immediately began operations along the west coast of Korea, striking at road and rail bridges, and on 13/14 October, Fireflies dive-bombed dockside installations. A second patrol from 29 October to 3 November proved uneventful, but the period from 5 to 26 December was very busy due to the Chinese crossing the border. Fireflies and Sea Furies attacked enemy convoys, vehicles, troop positions, bridges, and supply dumps.

Operating problems abounded. *Theseus* was in need of a hull cleaning and could only make twenty-two knots at best. A fully loaded Firefly FR.5 needed a wind of twenty knots along the deck to comfortably get airborne, and the Sea Fury needed twenty-eight knots, so on days of low wind the weapons load had to be reduced. To overcome this problem, Fireflies became bombers carrying 500- or 1,000-pound bombs, while the Sea Furies carried rockets, giving them a lighter load. The winter weather was frequently poor with intense cold, an icy flight deck, sea fog, and frequent gales. On 11 December 1950, MiG 15s attacked the ship's rescue helicopter, but skillful flying by the helicopter pilot avoided any damage.

From 25 January 1951, the 17th CAG operated off the west coast in support of the American 25th Division. Strikes were coordinated by USAF forward controllers flying unarmed North American T-6 trainers, known as 'Mosquito Flights.' Fully laden Fireflies were launched using RATO gear. These operations from *Theseus*, relieved on station at times by USS *Bataan* (CVL-29), continued strikes against enemy targets. Some aircraft were lost to light flak. By the time HMS *Glory* arrived on 22 April to relieve *Theseus*, the 17th CAG had flown 3,489 operational sorties.

Embarked in *Glory* were the 14th CAG, consisting of 812 Squadron with 12 Firefly FR.5s and 804 Squadron with 22 Sea Fury 11s. These continued to support United Nations troops. *Glory* was joined for a while in early May by USS *Bataan*, but the weather was poor and only a few sorties were flown. Any pause gave the Chinese time to repair bridges, which they did with local labor, usually overnight. To make certain strikes were more effective, some of the pilots flew lower and took their chances with the light flak, coming back to the carrier with bullet holes and shrapnel damage, plus pieces of earth and bits of their own rockets embedded in the tail. Another duty was spotting for ship-to-shore bombardments. Operations continued almost daily as the weather improved, and by 30 September, when *Glory* was relieved, the Fireflies had flown 1,055 operational sorties against approximately 3,000 targets.

Replacing *Glory* was the RAN carrier HMAS *Sydney* with 817 Squadron, which took over all the Fireflies of 812 Squadron before *Glory* left for the U.K. Joining them were Sea Fury 11s of 805 and 808 RAN Squadrons. Although the CAG system had been abandoned on 30 June 1951, *Sydney* had 21 CAG and part of 20 CAG embarked and retained the organization throughout her tour. Operational flying began on 5 October 1951 with three Firefly strikes, daily sorties against enemy targets continuing thereafter. On 14 October, Typhoon Ruth hit, and *Sydney* was subjected to waves reaching 45 feet in height and winds up to force twelve (over 70 knots). The ship rolled as much as 22 degrees. Six aircraft were complete write-offs with one Firefly swept overboard in a giant wave. After 'Ruth,' operations continued. On 23 October four USAF Boeing B-29s were shot down during a raid on northern airfields, two of them ditching north of Chodo, where a Firefly dropped a dinghy that saved at least one US airman. Throughout October and November strikes continued until 27 January 1952, when *Sydney* withdrew after launching 2,366 operational sorties while losing nine Fireflies, eight Sea Furies, and three pilots. Leaving Sasebo on 27 January 1952, *Sydney* sailed for Hong Kong where she rendezvoused with *Glory* and flew six Fireflies aboard the latter.

Glory arrived at Sasebo on 5 February 1952 with Fireflies of 812 Squadron and Sea Furies of 804 Squadron to join Task Element 95.12. Admiral Scott-Moncrieff, dissatisfied with the tasks given to his carrier aircraft, issued new directives which meant (▸▸ 44)

▲ **Large SEAC roundels are prominent on Firefly FR.1 DK438 ('277/N') of 1771 Squadron based aboard HMS *Implacable*. The last two digits of its side code are repeated on the radiator air intake. Above them is the name 'Lucy Quipment.'**

▾ **Observer Sub.Lt Val Bennett (left) and his pilot, Sub Lt Pete Kingston, about to climb into Firefly FR.1 '279' of 1772 Squadron aboard HMS *Indefatigable*. A rating has already opened the observer's cockpit hood. Bennett made a number of sketches showing the exploits of the squadron, as very few pictures were taken. The sketches were eventually displayed in the Board Room of the Fairey Aviation Co at Hayes in Middlesex, U.K.**

▾ **Two Fireflies, MB380 ('4A') and MB381 ('4B') of 1772 Squadron, formate over Schofields Airfield in Australia in March 1945. These are later model F.1s with raised windshields and cockpit canopies. No. 1772 Squadron replaced 1770 Squadron aboard HMS *Indefatigable* and flew operations against Japanese targets until the end of hostilities. They were the first British aircraft to fly over Tokyo since the beginning of World War II.**

43

▲ MB471 '280' of 1772 Squadron out on a reconnaissance sortie and carrying 45-gallon drop tanks. The fin flash has been painted out. Firefly 1s could carry either 45- or 90-gallon long-range tanks.

▼ Another unit too late to see action was 837 Squadron. Seen here are two of her Fireflies, '277' and '279/Y' (MB552), overflying their carrier, HMS *Glory*.

that the aircraft of *Glory* would in future take a much more aggressive role. Operations started on 7 February allowing area familiarization for new crews. The following day Fireflies used low-level skip bombing to deliver short-fused 500-pound bombs into two rail tunnels east of Changyon. On 8 February Fireflies again bombed a rail tunnel just north of Haeju, one bomb cutting the line and blocking the entrance. The next few days were spent helping ground forces by attacking enemy positions in villages, hayricks, and other buildings. US Navy carrier USS *Bairoko* (CVE-115) relieved *Glory* on 16 February and carried on attacks with F4U Corsairs, losing three, until 24 February when *Glory* returned. On 25 February Fireflies attacked the village of Chanyon and destroyed buildings at Yonchodo-ri. The weather that day turned completely overcast with thick clouds and poor visibility, and the Fireflies all landed back on *Glory* successfully using CCA (carrier controlled approach) techniques. The next day the Fireflies blocked another tunnel and damaged a bridge. The morning of 27 February found the Fireflies bombing road and rail bridges at Chearyong, and during the afternoon they dropped 1,000-pound bombs on enemy gun positions. At the end of the month aircrews were issued with a new, smaller Mae West and L-type dinghy pack — both popular because the former made it impossible to float face-down, while the latter was attached to the Mae West, so that the pilot did not have to retrieve it from the cockpit.

On 1 March, Fireflies bombed Changyon and strafed gun positions, villages, and supply warehouses. Over the next few days, the Fireflies continued their attacks on enemy supply lines. On 2 March, in poor weather, they attacked gun positions in the Chodo area and continued on to Chinnampo, where they attacked a North Korean naval headquarters scoring eight direct hits. On the way home at low level, they strafed enemy junks and sampans. Fireflies again blocked a tunnel north-east of Changyon, with four bombs seen to explode in the tunnel mouth. During this patrol, eight pilots celebrated achieving over one hundred operational sorties in the Korean theater. USS *Bairoko* took over on the evening of 4 March when *Glory* returned for replenishing and some replacement aircraft. Returning to the fray, *Glory* started operations again on 14 March by attacking enemy positions, but the weather during this patrol was poor, with gales and winds up to fifty knots.

Glory returned to Sasebo to replenish but was back on station on 1 April when Fireflies, using 500-pound bombs, breached a road bridge near Sochon. Bridges at Yonan and Hauju were Firefly targets on 2 April, and the next few days were spent attacking enemy positions including blocking another tunnel. On 9 April 812 Squadron attacked a road bridge and put it out of action, and others bombed a village that turned out to be a munitions depot, blowing it up in spectacular fashion.

Glory was again relieved by USS *Bairoko* on 9 April and after replenishment returned for her final patrol on 18 April. Despite low cloud and poor visibility, some sorties were flown against road bridges, enemy-held villages, and troop positions. The next few days were the same but on 22 April the Fireflies destroyed a village with the name Singsongdong! An ammunition factory north of Hauju was attacked by the Fireflies on 24 April, and another tunnel northwest of Changyon was bombed and blocked. A road bridge at Taetan was destroyed the following day. *Glory* now sailed for Hong Kong where her relief, HMS *Ocean*, was waiting. During *Glory*'s operations in Korean waters, the aircraft of 804 and 812 Squadrons had flown 4,835 operational sorties, losing twenty-seven aircraft and nine aircrew.

May saw the replacement of *Bairoko* by USS *Bataan*, which was to operate with *Ocean*. Aboard *Ocean* were thirty-one aircraft: Sea Fury FB.11s of 802 Squadron and Firefly FR.5s of 825 Squadron. The aircrew of both units were new to Korean operations. There was no shortage of targets, and attacks followed the familiar pattern of warehouses, road and rail stock, bridges, ammunition dumps, oil supplies, tunnels, and villages in the Ongjin, Chanyong,

Sinmak, Haeju, and Han River areas. A number of aircraft were lost, and those that ditched were usually picked up by the U.S. Navy. The rule on operations was "do not return for a second run," because by then the enemy had the line of flight zeroed in, and flak was intense. A Firefly pilot of 825 Squadron, hoping to help ground troops, made a second run and was shot down in flames on 19 May. Throughout May and June the attacks continued, on a daily basis if the weather allowed. On shorter trips the Fireflies carried a reduced fuel load with a full load of sixteen rockets, but on long-range missions with full fuel, the rocket load was reduced to twelve.

On 25 June, as the war entered its third year, the front lines were static, armistice negotiations were achieving nothing, and carrier aircraft strikes continued unabated. Three MiG-15s attacked a flight of four Fireflies of 825 Squadron on 27 June causing some damage; the MiGs, making only one pass, were not hit. One Firefly ditched, having also been hit by flak at the target area, and one force-landed on the beach at Paengyong-do. A short period for replenishment saw the arrival of two replacement Fireflies. Rocket projectiles were in short supply, and the ship left for her next patrol with only a thousand. To make full use of the Fireflies, their inboard rocket launchers were removed and bomb carriers installed so that they could carry two 1,000-pound or two 500-pound bombs or eight rockets. Operations resumed on 9 August when a flight of Sea Furies from 802 Squadron mixed it with eight MiG 15s, shooting down one MiG and damaging two others for no loss to themselves. The pilot of the Sea Fury was Lt. 'Hoagy' Carmichael with a unique distinction, at that time, of being the first FAA pilot of a piston-engine aircraft to shoot down a jet and the first to achieve an aerial victory for the FAA in the Korean War.

Fireflies continued to hit enemy targets, usually with bombs but sometimes with rockets. Not all squadron aircraft went to one target. Requests for strikes were prioritized as they came in, and it wasn't unusual for two Fireflies to bomb one target while others were sent elsewhere. More often than not, more than one target was attacked during such sorties; for instance, on 29 August, Fireflies struck in succession at six villages which were known to be harboring enemy troops and vehicles.

During replenishment, time-damaged aircraft were transferred to the support carrier HMS *Unicorn*, which provided replacement aircraft, so that 825 Squadron was restored to twelve Fireflies after each replenishment. *Ocean*'s next patrol was 26 August to 4 September, one Firefly ditching due to flak on the first day. Day after day, the carrier aircraft hit at enemy supply lines and positions. By September, *Ocean*'s aircraft were achieving an average of eighty-three sorties a day. Although the MiGs were in evidence at times, the USAF provided top cover with North American F-86 Sabres, and skirmishes were few. The intense flying continued until 4 November when *Ocean* withdrew to make way for *Glory*. Her aircraft had achieved 5,871 operational sorties using 420 1,000-pound bombs, 3,454 500-pound bombs, and 17,246 rockets and had fired nearly 825,000 rounds of 20 mm ammunition for a loss of seven Fireflies and nine Sea Furies.

Glory returned to the Korean theater for her third operational tour in November 1952 with thirteen Fireflies of 821 Squadron and twenty-one Sea Furies of 801 Squadron embarked. These were supplemented on 4 November when five Sea Furies, three Fireflies, and two S-51 Dragonfly helicopters were transferred from *Ocean*.

The air group aboard *Ocean* consisted of 810 Squadron with Fireflies and 807 Squadron with Sea Furies. Operations started on 22 May 1953 against enemy gun positions, buildings, troops, and communications. Targets were much the same as previous strikes, with a Firefly lost to ground fire on 29 June. The UN Command and communist forces agreed to negotiate an armistice on 8 July 1953, but on 13 July the Chinese launched another offensive against South Korean positions. It was during the negotiations that North Korean Po-2 biplanes flew over under cover of darkness to drop small fragmentation bombs on targets of opportunity, usually American bases. Attempts were made by F3D-2 Skynights and F4U Corsairs to (▶ 47)

▲ During the Korean War, replacement aircraft for squadrons were positioned at Sembawang on Singapore and transferred to carriers during the replenishment phase by ferrying them on across on the reserve and maintenance carrier HMS *Unicorn*. Here a Firefly FR.5 with UN identification stripes is hoisted aboard *Unicorn*. (IWM)

▶ Deck hands maneuver Firefly FR.5 WB408 to make more deck space. The long tail wheel arm made light work of such positioning. WB408 was serving with 810 Squadron aboard HMS *Theseus* and flew numerous strikes. It was damaged by flak on 12 March 1951 but survived and returned to the U.K. (IWM)

▲ Firefly FR.5 WB351 ('202/K') of 817 Squadron, aboard the Australian carrier HMAS *Sydney,* warms up prior to being launched on a strike. Due to the shortage of helicopters aboard British carriers, some were loaned by the US Navy. Whenever there was a launch the S-51 would take up a position off the port side in case of ditchings. (IWM)

▾ Armorers of 821 Squadron aboard HMS *Glory* work in non-military clothing to keep out the cold Korean winter as they winch up a 1,000-pound bomb on a Firefly's starboard wing. Zero-length rocket rails are installed between the bomb and fuel tank (replacing the ASH nacelle), and 20 mm ammunition hangs over the leading edge waiting to be fed into the belt feed mechanism of the wing guns.

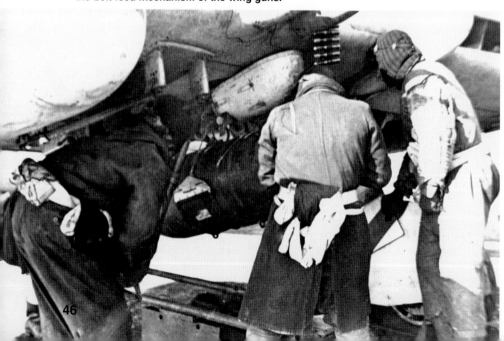

▲ Deck crew load 3-inch rocket projectiles under the wing of a Firefly FR.5 of 821 Squadron on HMS *Glory* in Korean waters. The rocket projectiles were painted dark green overall including the 60-pound heads. Loaded in tiers of two, they could be fired in pairs or as a salvo.

deter them, but these met with little success. In June 1953, 5th US Air Force Headquarters requested HMS *Ocean* to form a Firefly Night Fighter Detachment to combat the 'Bedcheck Charlies.' The detachment consisted of three Fireflies from 810 Squadron based ashore at Pyongtaek-ni. USAF GCI (ground controlled intercept) at Kimpo kept the Fireflies on a racetrack patrol between Inchon and Seoul directing them onto any 'target' not showing IFF signals. Over two hundred sorties were flown, and although no Po-2s were shot down once the patrols started, there were no more attacks by enemy intruders at night. The Fireflies returned to *Ocean* on 10 August 1953.

On 27 July 1953 the armistice agreement was signed and the guns fell silent. British and American carriers undertook flying and training missions off the west coast of Korea until the middle of September. HMS *Ocean's* final patrol in Korean waters was 12 to 16 October; she was withdrawn thereafter and sailed back to the U.K. During their time in Korea the ten FAA squadrons flew around 23,000 operational sorties losing twenty-six aircrew operationally and another seven in accidents.

Fireflies under Foreign Flags

Australia

The Royal Australian Navy (RAN) used Fireflies and Sea Furies to form their first CAG after World War II. On 28 August 1948, the RAN Fleet Air Arm formed the 20th CAG at Eglinton, Northern Island with No.816 Squadron operating the Firefly FR.5 and 805 Squadron operating the Hawker Sea Fury FB.11. The British Admiralty handed the carrier HMS *Terrible* over to the RAN who re-christened her HMAS *Sydney*. Embarking the 20th CAG, she sailed for Australia in April 1949. In November 1950, *Sydney* returned to the U.K. and there formed the 21st CAG consisting of No.817 Squadron with Firefly FR.5s and 808 Squadron with Sea Fury FB.11s. When they returned to Australia, the Air Group was joined by 805 Squadron equipped with Sea Fury FB.11s and sailed for Korean waters, where *Sydney* launched missions in support of United Nations ground forces between September 1951 and January 1952. Targets included rail bridges and tunnels, enemy gun positions, coastal shipping, road transport, troop positions, and other enemy targets. Despite appalling weather and heavy flak, Sydney's 21st Air Group achieved 2,366 operational sorties, the Fireflies flying 743 for a loss of three aircraft, plus two Sea Furies lost, with three pilots killed and one wounded. At least twenty-five aircraft were damaged by flak. The enthusiasm of some of the young pilots in pressing home their attacks could be measured by S/Lt. Rowland of 817 Squadron, who attacked at so low an altitude splinters from his bomb casing peppered his horizontal stabilizer. *Sydney* returned for a further tour of duty off Korea, but by then the Armistice had been signed and only peace-keeping patrols were flown.

The RAN eventually used 108 Fireflies in 816, 817, and 851 Squadrons (front-line) and 723, 724, and 725 Squadrons (training). Four Firefly FR.5s were converted into trainers with a raised rear cockpit, and two FR.5s were converted to target-towing duties followed by four Firefly AS.6 conversions to the target-towing role. The RAN operated two other carriers, HMS *Vengeance*, on loan from the Royal Navy when *Sydney* was in Korean waters, and HMAS *Melbourne,* acquired in 1949. Both operated Fireflies at different times. By the late 1950s, many of the Fireflies were suffering from fatigue, corrosion, and a general lack of spare parts, and the final ones were sold off in 1966.

(▶ 48)

▲ A pair of Firefly FR.5s from 810 Squadron formate for the camera. The squadron was based aboard HMS *Theseus* in 1951 and took part in the Korean War. Firefly '231/T' is WB417, and '235/T' is WB416, which survived the war and went on to become the prototype Firefly U.9 target drone. (IWM)

▼ Once hostilities ended in Korea on 27 July 1953, there was no need for identification stripes, so when HMAS *Sydney* arrived for its second tour of duty, its aircraft did not have them. These three Fireflies of 816 Squadron from *Sydney* patrol the Korean coast, the only markings of note being their red fins and upper rudders. (RAN)

Canada

The Royal Canadian Navy (RCN) operated sixty-four Fireflies: twenty-nine FR.1s, thirteen FR.4s, eighteen FR.5s, four T.1s, and two T.2s which were converted from two FR.1s. The FR.1s, all ex-FAA, were acquired between 1 June, 1946 and 10 April 1947. The equipment was the same as that of FAA aircraft except that the pilot's cockpit had a small radar scope fitted on the starboard side. Canadian FR.1s also had a TR5043 (SCR522) VHF radio located on a shelf directly behind the observer's seat.

The RCN's Fireflies were in continuous use by the RCN, both ashore and embarked in carriers, until the summer of 1950 when they were withdrawn and replaced by Grumman TBM-3E Avengers. The FR.4s were only on loan from the British Government pending the arrival of the AS.5, the first of these arriving on 12 February 1948 and the remainder on 24 May, 1948. Nine of these Fireflies were returned to Britain on 12 January, 1949, two having ditched at sea, and one was retained until March of 1954 before being returned to the U.K.

On 16 February 1949, the first Firefly AS.5s arrived. These differed from the British machines only in that they were fitted for AN/CRT-1 sonobuoy operation, along with the AN/ARR-3 receiver. When in use, the sonobuoys were slung in three clusters of four underneath the wings and/or fuselage. A sonobuoy receiver rod aerial projected downward from the bottom of the starboard center section. The AS.5s remained in use until November 1951 when they were replaced by Avengers.

Four Firefly T.1 trainers were obtained on 24 May 1948, the two FR.1 conversions to T.2 by the Fairey Aviation of Canada joining them in February 1950. All RCN Fireflies retained their original FAA serial numbers and were operated by 825 and 826 Squadrons with time embarked in carriers HMCS *Warrior* and *Magnificent*.

Denmark

In the summer of 1951, the Royal Danish Air Force (RDAF) ordered two Firefly TT.1 target towers. Fairey converted F.1s Z1842 and Z2020, which became '625' and '626' respectively and were delivered in October and November 1951. They were painted yellow overall with standard RDAF markings and serial number in black. Firefly '625' still had the low windshield of the earlier Firefly F.1s.

In 1952, the Royal Canadian Navy, under the Mutual Aid Military Assistance Program, presented four Firefly 1s to the RDAF. These were still in Mk.1 configuration and were converted for target towing duties using kits provided by Fairey Aviation and modified in the RDAF workshops at Vaerlose. The four were '627' (PP413), '628' (PP457), '629' (PP460), and '630' (MB579) and were painted the same as the first two. The Fireflies were used over the gunnery range off the Jutland coast, refuelling at Esbjerg being required due to the distance flown and sortie length. Three Fireflies ('627,' '628,' and '629') were written off in accidents, and in May 1959 the three remaining machines were sold to the Swedish target towing company, Svensk Flygtjanst, for Firefly fleet spares.

Ethiopia

The Imperial Ethiopian Air Force (IEAF) would have been one of the most prolific operators of the Firefly if their plans had gone through. Count von Rosen, the Swedish Commander-in-Chief of the IEAF, had tried to buy surplus Spitfires but was refused.

Sweden offered surplus F-51 Mustangs, but von Rosen wanted the Firefly, as he considered it a robust fighter-bomber more suitable for the harsh environment of Ethiopia. On 30 May 1950, Fairey Aviation informed the British Foreign Office von Rosen had told them he wanted thirty-five Fireflies, and that he would accept Mk.1s initially but was looking for trainers and later, Firefly FR.5s. Von Rosen ordered thirty-five Fireflies on 1 August 1950 to form a strike wing, but the Admiralty was reluctant to release that number of aircraft, especially when it was discovered they were to be used along the Eritrean border to put down terrorists.

Ethiopian Emperor Haille Selassie, obviously under pressure from von Rosen, informed Fairey Aviation that he would buy twelve new Firefly Mk5s straight off the production line. This was vetoed by the Admiralty, as all the Firefly FR.5s were needed by the Royal Navy, which was committed to supporting U.N. forces in the Korean War.

In December 1950, agreement was reached that thirty-five Firefly 1s would be reconditioned and sold in batches to the IEAF. The first batch of nine, eight FR.1s (601/MB434, 602/MB476, 604/MB497, 605/MB737, 606/Z2026, 607/Z2100, 608/Z1955 and 609/Z1982) plus one T.2 (603/MB382) were handed over in 1951. They were camouflaged in a cream and dark brown scheme with sky undersurfaces and red spinners.

No more Fireflies were delivered, the order being rescinded due to disagreements between the British Government and the IEAF. In March 1954, the IEAF bought 14 surplus Fireflies from the Canadian Government. These were nine FR.1s (DK535, DK537, DK545, DK560, DK561, DK565, PP402, PP462, and PP467), three T.1s (DK445, DT975, and MB443) and two T.2s (MB694 and PP408). These were delivered in the RCN color scheme with the Canadian roundels being replaced by those of the Ethiopian Air Force. Identification was by a large number across the fin and rudder in black, e.g. '612.' The Fireflies were used operationally along the borders of the Sudan and Somalia to quell terrorists. There were rumors that the IEAF also had acquired some surplus Fireflies from the Dutch, but there is no evidence that they were delivered.

When withdrawn from use, the surviving Fireflies, most of which had less than five hundred hours on them, were inhibited and stored in a hangar at Asmara. They were later pushed out in the sun and languished on the airfield for thirty years. Four were acquired by museums in the mid-1990s; two went to South Africa, one to the National Aviation Museum, Ottawa, and the other to CFB Shearwater Aviation Museum, Nova Scotia.

India

In 1953, the Indian Navy approached Fairey Aviation and bought five Firefly TT.1s. These were delivered during June/July of 1954 in overall silver finish on the upper surfaces and black-and-yellow striped undersurfaces. Standard Indian roundels and fin flashes were applied to the wings, fuselage, and fin. Serial numbers in black were (with previous FAA identity) INS111 (DK566), INS112 (DK477), INS113 (PP488), INS114 (DK479), and INS115 (DK552).

Five Firefly TT.4s were ordered in 1956 and delivered in 1958. These were in the same markings as for the TT.1s with serials INS116 (VG964), INS117 (VG985), INS118 (TW749), INS119 (VH128) and INS120 (VG980). By the early 1960s, maintenance and spares were becoming a problem, so nine were withdrawn and sold for scrap, with one retained for a planned museum. Not all the bits went into the melting pot; the Firefly currently under restoration in the United States contains parts from India.

Netherlands

In 1945, the Royal Netherlands Naval Air Service bought thirty new Firefly F.1s from Fairey Aviation with first deliveries taking place in January 1946. These came off the production line at Hayes camouflaged the same as FAA Fireflies except for an inverted orange triangle positioned just forward of the pilot's cockpit and one high up on the rudder. The first fifteen Fireflies delivered became No.860 Squadron and embarked on HNMS *Karel Doorman*, the ex-British carrier HMS *Nairana*. They sailed to the Dutch East Indies where the Fireflies went ashore at Kemajoran airfield, Java. This was a time of unrest, with the local population wanting independence from the Dutch. In what became an irresolvable problem, the Dutch tried to put the rebellion down using force. Operating mainly from the bases at Morokrembangan and Soerabaja, the Fireflies went into action, flying operational sorties in support of the Dutch Marines and Army using rockets and cannon. Most of the sorties were flown by a single pilot, there being hardly any need for an observer/navigator.

It was 1951 before hostilities ceased and the Dutch East Indies became Indonesia, by which time the Fireflies had flown almost continuous operations in over four thousand sorties, two being lost to ground fire and two in accidents. No.860 Squadron returned to Holland with eleven Fireflies. Some of the other fifteen were used by 861 Squadron and 1 Squadron in the Netherland Antilles. Seven F.1s were later converted into Firefly trainers. In the meantime, during late 1946 the RNNAS had ordered forty new Firefly FR.4s to supplement the F.1s, these being delivered between April and December 1947. They served with 2, 4, and 5 Squadrons in Holland, 1 Squadron in the Netherlands Antilles, and 7 Squadron at Biak, Netherlands New Guinea. Of these, nine were lost in accidents, and eight were converted to target-towers, with about seven surviving until 1961.

Early in 1949, the Royal Netherlands Navy, as it had become, bought fourteen new Firefly NF.5s, seven of which survived until 1961 when all Dutch Fireflies were withdrawn from use. In service the FR.4s and NF.5s used the same paint scheme as that of the FAA but with Dutch roundels. The Dutch side codes became quite complicated and on some aircraft were changed at least five times! Later aircraft had 'KON. MARINE' stencilled on the rear fuselage under the horizontal stabilizer.

Sweden

In 1948 Svensk Flygjanst AB, a private Swedish company that provided target towing facilities for the Swedish armed forces, was looking for a suitable replacement for its aging Miles Martinets. The Firefly had proved to be an ideal aircraft for such duties. It cruised relatively fast at 200 knots; its airframe and engine were well proven; it had a rear cockpit for drogue operator; and because it was a surplus military aircraft, its cost was low. Sixteen were eventually ordered and delivered between December 1948 and 1951. They were SE-BRA/DK568, SE-BRB/DK459, SE-BRC/Z1908, SE-BRD/Z2033, SE-BRF/DT986, SE-BRG/DT989, SE-BRH/MB387, SE-BRI/DV121, SE-BRK/MB503, SE-BRL/DT939, SE-BRM/DK430, SE-BYB/MB624, SE-BYC/MB728, SE-BYD/MB702, SE-CAU/PP469, and SE-CAW/PP392, plus three aircraft from Denmark, which were registered SE-CHL/RDAF 625, SE-CHM/RDAF 626, and SE-CHN/RDAF 630, but never flew in those markings. During their time with Svensk, the Fireflies accumulated 14,962 flying hours before all remaining Firefly TT.1s were withdrawn from use in 1964. SE-BRD was presented to the Skyfame Museum in the U.K., flying there on 5 May 1964. Skyfame later became part of the Imperial War Museum collection at Duxford, and SE-BRD later moved to the Fleet Air Arm Museum at Yeovilton where it is still on display. Two others were presented to Swedish museums.

▲ The Royal Thai Air Force (RTAF) operated Firefly FR.1s against border terrorists. This one, 'SF.1,' is armed with two 1,000-pound (454 kg) bombs and zero-length rocket rail mounts. Red spinners were standard, and Thai national markings included a Thai flag on the rudder.

Thailand

In the post-World War II era, the Royal Thailand Navy wanted to expand and form its own air arm in order to become independent of the Royal Thai Air Force (RTAF). Impressed by its operational history and strike capability, Thai naval officials ordered ten Firefly FR.1s (SF1/MB469, SF2/MB445, SF3/DK483, SF4/MB407, SF5/MB494, SF7/DT931, SF8/MB439, SF10/MB435, SF11/MB410, and SF12/Z2102) and two T.2s (SF6/Z2037 and SF9/MB750). These were painted Dark Sea Grey on the upper surfaces with Sky undersurfaces and fuselage sides as on FAA aircraft. Spinners were red. Thai roundels were applied to the wings but the fuselage marking was an anchor in black. Crated, they were delivered by sea to Bangkok in November 1951. However, by then the Thai Navy had tried to effect a *coup d'état* and failed, and the Fireflies were transferred to the Royal Thai Air Force base at Don Muang and RTAF roundels replaced the anchors on the fuselage. Operated by No.1 Squadron of the IV Wing, they were used operationally along the borders until 1954 when they were retired, one (SF11) being retained in the RTAF Museum at Bangkok.

Others

Other services interested in obtaining Fireflies included the Argentine Navy (Firefly FR.4s), Afghanistan Air Force (Firefly FR.4), French Navy (Firefly FR.4), Finnish Air Force (Firefly Mk.1 or 4), Royal Iraqi Air Force (Firefly FR.4), Egyptian Air Force (Firefly FR.4), Lebanese Air Force (Firefly FR.5), Saudi Arabian Air Force (Firefly FR.5), and Syrian Air Force (Firefly FR.1/FR.4). However, various obstacles, usually in the form of objections from the FAA and/or the Admiralty, intervened to thwart these foreign purchases.

Get Hooked!
More naval aircraft from Squadron/Signal Publications

1097 TBD Devastator

1122 SBU Vindicator

1214 F/A-18 Hornet

1175 Fairey Swordfish

1191 F4F Wildcat

5504 F4F Wildcat

5509 F6F Hellcat

5525 TBF/TBM Avenger

5533 SBD Dauntless

For more information on Squadron/Signal books, visit www.SquadronSignalPublications.co